AMPHITRYON

ALSO BY RICHARD WILBUR

The Beautiful Changes and Other Poems
Ceremony and Other Poems
A Bestiary (editor, with Alexander Calder)
Molière's *The Misanthrope* (translator)
Things of This World
Poems 1943–1956
Candide (with Lillian Hellman)
Poe: Complete Poems (editor)
Advice to a Prophet and Other Poems
Molière's *Tartuffe* (translator)
The Poems of Richard Wilbur
Loudmouse (for children)
Shakespeare: Poems (co-editor, with Alfred Harbage)
Walking to Sleep: New Poems and Translations
Molière's *The School for Wives* (translator)
Opposites
The Mind-Reader: New Poems
Responses: Prose Pieces, 1948–1976
Molière's *The Learned Ladies* (translator)
Racine's *Andromache* (translator)
Racine's *Phaedra* (translator)
New and Collected Poems
More Opposites
Molière's *The School for Husbands* and
Sganarelle, or The Imaginary Cuckold (translator)

JEAN BAPTISTE POQUELIN DE

AMPHITRYON

TRANSLATED INTO ENGLISH VERSE
AND WITH AN AFTERWORD BY
RICHARD WILBUR

HARCOURT BRACE & COMPANY
NEW YORK SAN DIEGO LONDON

Requests for permission to make copies of any part of the work should be mailed to: Permissions Department, Harcourt Brace & Company, 6277 Sea Harbor Drive, Orlando, Florida 32887-6777.

Portions of this translation first appeared in the magazine *Metamorphoses* and in the newsletter of the Princeton University Library.

Caution: Professionals and amateurs are hereby warned that these translations, being fully protected under the copyright laws of the United States of America, the British Empire, including the Dominion of Canada, and all other countries which are signatories to the Universal Copyright Convention and the International Copyright Union, are subject to royalty. All rights, including professional, amateur, motion picture, recitation, lecturing, public reading, radio broadcasting, and television, are strictly reserved. Particular emphasis is laid on the question of readings, permission for which must be secured from the author's agent in writing. Inquiries on professional rights (except for amateur rights) for *Amphitryon* should be addressed to Mr. Gilbert Parker, William Morris Agency, 1350 Avenue of the Americas, New York, NY 10019. Inquiries on translation rights should be addressed to: Permissions Department, Harcourt Brace & Company, 6277 Sea Harbor Drive, Orlando, Florida 32887-6777.

The amateur acting rights of this translation are controlled exclusively by the Dramatists Play Service, Inc., 440 Park Avenue South, New York, NY 10016. No amateur performance of the play may be given without obtaining in advance the written permission of the Dramatists Play Service, Inc., and paying the requisite fee.

Library of Congress Cataloging-in-Publication Data
Molière, 1622–1673.
    [Amphitryon. English]
    Amphitryon/Jean Baptiste Poquelin de Molière; translated into English verse and with an afterword by Richard Wilbur.
        p.   cm.
    "A Harvest original."
    ISBN 0-15-100156-1.—ISBN 0-15-600211-6 (pbk.)
    1. Amphitryon (Greek mythology)—Drama.   I. Wilbur, Richard, 1921–   . II. Title.
PQ1827.A7E513   1995
842'.4—dc20   94-40640

Printed in the United States of America
First edition
A B C D E

For Bill and Sonja

Amphitryon

COMEDY IN THREE ACTS, 1668

CHARACTERS

MERCURY, messenger of the Gods

NIGHT, a goddess

JUPITER (JOVE), in the guise of Amphitryon

MERCURY, in the guise of Sosia

AMPHITRYON (*am-FIT-ree-un*), general of the Thebans

ALCMENA (*alk-MEE-na*), Amphitryon's wife

CLEANTHIS (*clee-AN-this*), lady's maid to Alcmena, and wife of Sosia

ARGATIPHONTIDAS (*ar-gah-tee-FON-tee-das*), NAUCRATES, POLIDAS, POSICLES: Theban captains

SOSIA (*SO-see-uh*), Amphitryon's manservant

The scene: Thebes, in front of Amphitryon's house

PROLOGUE

MERCURY, *on a cloud;* NIGHT, *in a chariot drawn through the air by two horses*

MERCURY

Whoa, charming Night! I beg you, stop and tarry.
There is a favor I would ask of you.
      I bring you a word or two
      As Jupiter's emissary.

NIGHT

    So it's you, Lord Mercury! Heaven knows,
I scarcely knew you in that languid pose.

MERCURY

Ah me! I was so weary and so lame
From running errands at great Jove's behest,
I sat down on a little cloud to rest
      And wait until you came.

NIGHT

Oh, come now, Mercury. Is it proper for
A god to say that he is tired and sore?

[*Prologue*]

Are we made of iron?

                    No; but we must maintain
A tone befitting our divinity.
Some words, if uttered by the gods, profane
    Our lofty rank and high degree,
    And such base language ought to be
Restricted to the human plane.

    That's easy enough for you to say;
You have, my sweet, a chariot and a pair
Of splendid steeds to whisk you everywhere
In a most nonchalant and queenly way.
    But my life's not like that at all;
And, given my unjust and dismal fate,
    I owe the poets endless hate
    For their unutterable gall
    In having heartlessly decreed,
    Ever since Homer sang of Troy,
    That each god, for his use and need,
    Should have a chariot to enjoy,
    While I must go on foot, indeed,
    Like some mere village errand boy—
I, who in Heaven and on earth am known
As the famed messenger of Jove's high throne,
    And who, without exaggeration,
    Considering all the chores I'm given,
    Need, more than anyone in Heaven,
    To have some decent transportation.

NIGHT

Too bad, but there's no help for it;
The poets treat us as they please.
There's no end to the idiocies
That those fine gentlemen commit.
Still, you are wrong to chide them so severely:
They gave you wingèd heels; that's quite a gift.

MERCURY

Oh, yes: they've made my feet more swift,
But does that make my legs less weary?

NIGHT

Lord Mercury, your point is made.
Now, what's this message that you bear?

MERCURY

It comes from Jove, as you're aware.
He wishes you to cloak him with your shade
    While, in a gallant escapade,
    He consummates a new affair.
To you, Jove's habits can be nothing new;
You know how often he forsakes the skies;
How much he likes to put on human guise
When there are mortal beauties to pursue,
    And how he's full of tricks and lies
    That purest maids have yielded to.
Alcmena's bright eyes lately turned his head;
And while, upon the far Boeotian plain,
    Amphitryon, her lord, has led
    His Thebans in a fierce campaign,

7

[*Prologue*]

Jove's taken his form and, acting in his stead,
    Is eased now of his amorous pain
By the soft pleasures of the lady's bed.
It serves his purpose that the couple were
But lately married; and the youthful heat
Of their amours, their ardor keen and sweet,
Were what inclined the crafty Jupiter
    To this particular deceit.
His tactic has succeeded, in this case:
    Though, doubtless, such impersonations
Would, with most wives, be vain and out of place;
It isn't always that her husband's face
    Will give a woman palpitations.

NIGHT

Jove baffles me, and I have trouble seeing
Why these impostures give him such delight.

MERCURY

He likes to sample every state of being,
And in so doing he's divinely right.
However high the rôle that men assign him,
    I'd not think much of him if he
Forever played the awesome deity
And let the jeweled bounds of Heaven confine him.
It is, I think, the height of silly pride
Always to be imprisoned in one's splendor;
Above all, if one would enjoy the tender
Passions, one must set one's rank aside.
Jove is a connoisseur of pleasures, who

Is practiced in descending from on high;
When he would enter into any new
      Delight, he lays his selfhood by,
And Jupiter the god is lost to view.

NIGHT

One might excuse his leaving our high station
To mix with mankind in a lower place,
And sample human passions, however base,
      And share men's foolish agitation,
If only, in his taste for transformation,
He'd join no species save the human race.
      But for great Jupiter to change
      Into a bull, or swan, or snake,
      Is most unsuitable and strange,
And causes tongues to cluck and heads to shake.

MERCURY

      Let critics carp, in their conceit:
      Such metamorphoses are sweet
      In ways they cannot comprehend.
Jove knows what he's about, in all his dealings;
And in their passions and their tender feelings,
Brutes are less brutish than some folk contend.

NIGHT

Let us revert to the current lady-friend.
If Jove's sly trick has proved auspicious,
What does he ask of me? What more can he need?

[*Prologue*]

MERCURY

That you rein in your horses, check their speed,
And thereby satisfy his amorous wishes,
  Stretching a night that's most delicious
  Into a night that's long indeed;
That you allow his fires more time to burn,
And stave the daylight off, lest it awaken
   The man whose place he's taken,
   And hasten his return.

NIGHT

 It's not the prettiest of tasks
 That Jupiter would have me do!
 There's a sweet name for creatures who
 Perform the service that he asks!

MERCURY

 For a young goddess, you embrace
 Old-fashioned notions, it seems to me;
 To do such service isn't base
 Except in those of low degree.
When one is blessed with high estate and standing,
  All that one does is good as gold,
  And things have different names, depending
  On what position one may hold.

NIGHT

 In matters of this dubious kind
 You've more experience than I;

[*Prologue*]

I'll trust your counsel, then, and try
To do this thing that Jove's assigned.

MERCURY

Ho! Dearest Madam Night, take care;
Don't overdo it, pray; go easy.
Your reputation everywhere
Is not for being prim and queasy.
In every clime, you've played a shady part
    In many a tryst and rendezvous;
As far as morals are concerned, dear heart,
        There's little to choose between us two.

NIGHT

Enough. Let's cease to bicker thus;
    Let us maintain our dignities,
And let's not prompt mankind to laugh at us
    By too much frankness, if you please.

MERCURY

Farewell. I must descend now, right away,
And, putting off the form of Mercury,
    So change that I may seem to be
        Amphitryon's valet.

NIGHT

I shall ride on but, as you ask of me,
    I'll often dawdle and delay.

[*Prologue*]

Good day, dear Night.

Good Mercury, good day.

(*Mercury alights from his cloud, and
Night traverses the stage in her chariot.*)

ACT ONE

SCENE ONE

SOSIA

SOSIA

Who goes there? At each step, I quake and cower!
    Sirs, I'm a friend to everyone.
    Oh, what a dreadful risk I run,
    Walking abroad at such an hour!
    My master, having won his fight,
    Has charged me with this perilous labor.
If he felt an ounce of charity toward his neighbor,
Would he send me out into so black a night?
To have me herald his return, and say
    The praises of his victory, might
He not have waited for the break of day?
    Behold, poor Sosia, how you are
    Mistreated in your servile state!
    The lot of underlings is far
    More cruel when those we serve are great.
We lesser creatures are designed, they hold,
    To serve their whims until we drop.
By day or night, in wind, hail, heat, or cold,
    They've but to speak, and we must hop.
    With them, long years of servitude
    Will never stand us in good stead.
    Their least caprice, or shift of mood,
    Brings down their wrath upon our head.
    Yet foolishly we cling and cleave

15

To the empty honor of being at their side,
And strive to feel what other men believe,
That we are privileged and full of pride.
In vain our reason bids us quit our place;
In vain, resentment counsels us the same;
      But when we stand before their face,
      They cow us and deflect our aim,
And their least nod, or smile, or show of grace
      Renders us dutiful and tame.
      But now at last, through this dark night,
I see our house, and all my terrors flee.
      I need, for this my embassy,
      Some polished speech I can recite.
I owe Alcmena a tale of martial glory—
Of how our forces thrashed the foe for fair;
      But how can I recount that story
      When, after all, I wasn't there?
No matter; I'll tell of blows and counterblows
      As if I'd witnessed all the fray.
How often battles are described by those
      Who played it safe and stayed away!
      I must rehearse a bit, and groom
      Myself to give this rôle my best.
Let's say that this is the reception room;
      This lantern is Alcmena, to whom
      My eloquence must be addressed.
    (*Sosia places his lantern on the ground, and addresses it.*)
Amphitryon, Madam, my master and your mate,
(Well turned!) whose thoughts are ever of your charms,
      Has chosen me as his delegate
To bring you news of his success in arms,
And say how much he's longed for you of late.
      "Ah, Sosia! My heart's aglow
      With joy to see you back again!"
      I'm the most fortunate of men,

    Madam, if you esteem me so.
(Good answer!) "Tell me how Amphitryon does."
    Madam, he does as brave men do
Whenever there is glory to pursue.
       (Ha! As pretty a speech as ever was!)
"But when will he return, that glorious man,
    And make my happiness entire?"
Madam, he'll come as quickly as he can,
Though far less quickly than he would desire.
(Ha!) "Into what state of mind has the war led him?
How does he speak, or act? I long to know."
Madam, he'd sooner act than speak, and so
    His enemies have cause to dread him.
(Listen to that! Am I not the prince of wits?)
"Have the rebels met the fate they merited?"
They couldn't withstand us, Madam, and as they fled
    We followed, cutting them to bits;
    Their leader, Pterelas, is dead,
And Telebos is taken; it is said
    That everywhere the foe submits.
"My heavens! Who dreamt of a success so great?
Tell me, good Sosia, how the battle went."
Well, Madam, not to brag or overstate,
    I can with certainty relate
    The details of that great event.
    Suppose that Telebos is here,
    Madam—that on this side it lies.
  (*Sosia indicates the locations on his hand, or on the ground.*)
    It is a city which, in size,
    Is big as Thebes, or very near.
       Here's where the river flows.
       This was our camping place,
       While, over there, our foes
       Had occupied that space.
       Up there, upon a height,

17

Was their infantry in force;
Lower, and to the right,
Was a regiment of horse.
Once we'd addressed our prayers to the gods,
The word came down to engage the enemy.
Our foes, who thought at once to seize the odds,
Sent forth, in three platoons, their cavalry;
But soon we damped their ardor and their zest,
            As I shall now expound.
Here came our vanguard, keen to do their best;
        Here were the royal archers found;
            And here our main force pressed—
                (*A noise is heard, from offstage.*)
Forward . . . But wait, that force has had a scare;
        I hear, it seems to me, a noise.

SCENE TWO

MERCURY, *coming out of Amphitryon's house,*
in the guise of Sosia

Disguised as that damned babbler there,
  I'll drive him off ere he destroys
The quiet of this night, and mars the joys
  Now savored by our loving pair.

SOSIA, *not seeing Mercury*

No further noises trouble me;
  My fears are somewhat pacified.
But, just in case, my colloquy
  Had best be finished up inside.

MERCURY, *aside*

Unless you're stronger than Mercury,
  Your entry's going to be denied.

SOSIA, *not seeing Mercury*

What a long night! How slow its hours creep!
Given the time I've traveled, trudging on,
My master must have mistaken dusk for dawn,

Or fair-haired Phoebus, having drunk too deep,
    Must lie abed and oversleep.

MERCURY, *aside*

    Just listen to that knave defame
    A deity! What irreverence!
    My arm shall punish him at once,
    Leaving him sore in all his frame;
And I'll have sport by stealing from the dunce
Not only his appearance but his name.

SOSIA, *perceiving Mercury from a distance*

    Oh, horrors! My anxiety
    Was just; my goose is cooked. Look there!
    Before my master's house I see
    A person whose forbidding air
    Is not a pleasant augury.
    I think, to cover up my fears,
    That I shall sing a bar or two.
              (*He sings.*)

MERCURY

Now who, I wonder, is this scoundrel who
Presumes to sing, and to torment my ears?
   (*As Mercury speaks, Sosia's voice grows gradually weaker.*)
Perhaps he'd like my fists to work him over?

SOSIA, *aside*

The man, it seems, is not a music lover.

MERCURY

For longer than a week,
I've not had anybody's skull to crack;
My muscles, from disuse, have all grown slack;
    I need to break somebody's back,
    So as to build up my physique.

SOSIA, *aside*

    My gods! What sort of fiend is this?
I feel so terrified that I could die.
    But let's not show our cowardice
By trembling; he may be as scared as I.
    Such threats may be mere artifice
To hide his inner panic from my eye.
Yes, yes, I mustn't play the frightened mouse.
Though I'm not brave, I can dissimulate.
    Come, rise above this timid state:
The man's alone; I'm strong; my master's great,
        And here's my master's house.

MERCURY

Who goes there?

SOSIA

        I.

MERCURY

    Who?

21

[*Act One • Scene Two*]

SOSIA

I. (*Aside:*) Bold repartee!

MERCURY

What are you?

SOSIA

I am a man, and so can talk.

MERCURY

Are you master, or servant?

SOSIA

Whichever I choose to be.

MERCURY

Where are you going?

SOSIA

Wherever my feet may walk.

MERCURY

Your tone annoys me.

SOSIA

How that pleases me!

[*Act One • Scene Two*]

Wretch, I shall make you tell me—and I can,
　　Despite your insolence and nerve—
Whither you travel tonight, whence you began,
　　What you are doing, and whom you serve.

SOSIA

　I do both good and ill with verve;
Come here, go there; and am my master's man.

MERCURY

You show some wit, and I can see you're out
To seem a person of superior kind.
To celebrate our meeting, I feel inclined
　　To give your head a little clout.

SOSIA

You'd strike me?

MERCURY

　　Yes. Here, lest you be in doubt.
　　(*Mercury gives Sosia a blow.*)

SOSIA

Ow! That was done in earnest.

MERCURY

　　　　No, in fun,
And in response to all your joking.

23

SOSIA

My gods, friend! How you batter one!
I'd not said anything provoking.

MERCURY

That blow was the gentlest I can do,
One of my modest little taps.

SOSIA

Had I not more restraint than you,
We'd have an ugly scene, perhaps.

MERCURY

You've not seen anything as yet;
We'll do far better, by and by.
For now, however, let's you and I
Resume our little tête-à-tête.

SOSIA

I quit.

(*Sosia starts to leave.*)

MERCURY, *stopping Sosia*

Just tell me where you're going.

SOSIA

What for?

[*Act One • Scene Two*]

MERCURY

Come, where are you going? I wish to know.

SOSIA

I'm going to knock upon that door.
What moves you to detain me so?

MERCURY

If you go near that door, you're going to get
A storm of buffets for your impudence.

SOSIA

You mean to keep me, by that threat,
From entering our residence?

MERCURY

"Our residence," eh?

SOSIA

Our residence, yes.

MERCURY

What rot!
You're of that household, so you say.

SOSIA

Of course. It's Amphitryon's household, is it not?

[*Act One • Scene Two*]

MERCURY

How does that prove your statement, pray?

SOSIA

I'm his man.

MERCURY

You?

SOSIA

I.

MERCURY

His servant?

SOSIA

I am, sincerely.

MERCURY

Amphitryon's servant?

SOSIA

His servant, without a doubt.

MERCURY

And your name's? . . .

[*Act One • Scene Two*]

SOSIA

Sosia.

MERCURY

How's that?

SOSIA

Sosia.

MERCURY

Now, hear me:
Do you know that this fist is itching to knock you out?

SOSIA

What for? What gives you such a fierce intention?

MERCURY

Tell me, presumptuous rascal, what on earth
Moved you to take the name you mention?

SOSIA

I didn't take it; it's been mine from birth.

MERCURY

What insolence! What brazen falsity!
You dare maintain that Sosia is your name!

[*Act One • Scene Two*]

SOSIA

Indeed I so maintain, because the same
Was given me by the gods' supreme decree;
It's something I've no power to disclaim;
    I can't be someone else than me.

MERCURY

You've earned a thousand cudgel strokes, you whelp,
    By all of these effronteries.

SOSIA, *being beaten by Mercury*

Justice, citizens, justice! Save me, please!

MERCURY

So, dog, you whine and cry for help!

SOSIA

Do you expect me not to yelp,
When you deal me a thousand blows like these?

MERCURY

I thrash you thus . . .

SOSIA

        It's a tawdry thing to do.
   You take advantage of my lack
Of courage, to abuse my smarting back,

28

And that is most unfair of you.
It's bullying, pure and simple, when
A man takes pleasure in belaboring men
    Too craven to retaliate.
To trounce a coward earns one no bravos;
    And to prove one's pluck by bashing those
    Who have none, is a sorry trait.

MERCURY

Well, are you Sosia still? What do you say?

SOSIA

Your blows have caused no metamorphosis
In me, and the sole effect of all of this
    Is that I'm Sosia *frappé.*

MERCURY, *threatening to beat him again*

Such quips will cost you a hundred strokes apiece.

SOSIA

Ah, cease your blows, for the love of heaven.

MERCURY

Then let your insolent prattle cease.

SOSIA

Just as you wish; I'll gladly hold my peace,
For this debate of ours is most uneven.

[*Act One • Scene Two*]

MERCURY

Are you Sosia still? . . . Speak out, if you wish to live!

SOSIA

I'll be whatever you insist.
Make of me what you will. Your arm and fist
    Have gained you that prerogative.

MERCURY

So you thought that you were Sosia, in the past?

SOSIA

Yes, until now the matter seemed quite plain;
    But the recent teachings of your cane
    Have shown me my mistake at last.

MERCURY

It's I who am Sosia, as all Thebes knows.
Amphitryon's had no other man but me.

SOSIA

You're . . . Sosia?

MERCURY

Yes, I'm Sosia! And he
Who mocks my claim will risk a broken nose.

[*Act One • Scene Two*]

SOSIA, *aside*

Must I renounce myself, then, and stand by
While this impostor steals my very name?
    It's fortunate for him that I
    Was born so timid and so tame,
For otherwise, by Jove . . .

MERCURY

                You're muttering through
Your teeth; is there some meaning in it?

SOSIA

No; but, by all the gods, I beg of you
    That I may speak to you for a minute.

MERCURY

Speak, then.

SOSIA

          But promise me, I pray,
That you'll not beat me in reply.
Let's sign a truce.

MERCURY

          Come, say your say.
Your truce I hereby ratify.

[*Act One • Scene Two*]

SOSIA

Tell me, what put this mad whim into your head?
What use is my name to you, for Heaven's sake?
And, even if you were a demon, how could you make
Me not myself, but someone else instead?

MERCURY, *raising his stick*

So! Once again, you—

SOSIA

                    Wait! Take care!
To break our truce would not be fair.

MERCURY

You weasel, you impostor! . . .

SOSIA

                    As for such
Harsh names, you may apply them
Freely; they don't hurt much,
And I'm not bothered by them.

MERCURY

You say that you're Sosia?

SOSIA

                    Yes. All this absurd . . .

MERCURY

Watch out: I'll break our truce—take back my word—

SOSIA

No matter. I can't annul myself for you,
Or listen to more fantasy and sham.
How can you be the person that I am?
        Can I cease to be myself? Not true!
Has anyone ever heard of such a thing?
Can one dismiss a sea of evidence?
        Am I dreaming? Am I slumbering?
Have visions addled my intelligence?
        Am I not coolly reasoning,
        And wide awake in every sense?
Was I not ordered by Amphitryon
To come here where his bride, Alcmena, lives,
Convey his love in warm superlatives,
And tell her of the martial deeds he's done?
Did I not walk here from the port, of late?
        Is not a lantern in my hand?
Did I not find you here before our gate?
Was not my manner courteous and bland?
Did you not then exploit my cowardice,
        And bar my entrance to our dwelling?
Have you not thrashed me with such emphasis
        That my back's bruised beyond all telling?
All that I've said is all too true, alas;
        I would to Heaven it were not!
Cease to abuse a poor wretch. Let me pass
To do the humble duties which are my lot.

[*Act One • Scene Two*]

MERCURY

Halt! If you take one step, it will attract
The lightning of my wrath to strike your spine.
    The tale you've told me is, in fact,
    Save for the blows, entirely mine.
'Twas I who, as Amphitryon's deputy,
Arrived this very minute from the coast;
I who shall greet Alcmena, and shall boast
Of how her brave lord brought us victory,
And slew the leader of the enemy host.
I'm Sosia, I may say with certitude,
    Son of the shepherd Davus, and
Brother of Harpax, dead in a foreign land;
    Husband, moreover, of the prude
    Cleanthis, whose moods I cannot stand;
I have been flogged in Thebes full many a time
    For deeds of which I shall not speak,
And branded on my backside for the crime
    Of getting caught at . . . hide-and-seek.

SOSIA, *sotto voce, aside*

He's right. Except by *being* Sosia, how
Could he know so much? And it's truthful, all of it!
This fellow's words astonish me, and now
I'm starting to believe the man a bit.
What's more, as I look closer now, I see
That he has my bearing, shape, and countenance.
    I'll ask him a question which, perchance,
    May clarify this mystery.
                (*Aloud:*)
Out of the booty taken from our foes,
What did Amphitryon choose as his fair share?

MERCURY

Five massive diamonds were what he chose,
Set in a brooch their chief was wont to wear.

SOSIA

Who shall receive this gift so richly wrought?

MERCURY

His wife, to complement her glowing charms.

SOSIA

In what container shall the gift be brought?

MERCURY

A casket, sealed with my master's coat-of-arms.

SOSIA, *aside*

There's not one lie in all of his discourse,
And I feel shaken. He has already made me
Admit that he is Sosia by brute force;
Now reason, too, seems likely to persuade me.
Yet when I pinch myself, or calmly ponder,
    It seems to me that I am I.
Is there not some decisive test, I wonder,
    That I can be enlightened by?
Yes! What I've done when no one was around
Cannot be known, of course, unless by me!
I've thought now of a question which is bound
To stump him altogether. We shall see.

[*Act One • Scene Two*]

(Aloud:)
During the battle, you hid in the Theban tents.
What did you do there, while you waited?

MERCURY

From a ham . . .

SOSIA, aside

That's it!

MERCURY

. . . which I'd appropriated,
I bravely cut two slices, both immense,
    On which I gorged till I was sated.
I washed them down with someone's rare old wine
Which, ere I sipped it, gave my eyes delight,
    And drank a toast to our battle line,
    Wishing them courage in the fight.

SOSIA, aside

This final test appears to settle
The question quite conclusively;
The man could not have spied on me,
Unless he was inside the bottle.
(Aloud:)
After these proofs you've given, I can't deny
That you are Sosia; to that I'll say amen.
But if you're he, tell me who *I* am, then—
Because I must be someone, mustn't I?

36

MERCURY

When I am Sosia no more,
   You may be he; I think that's fair.
But while I'm he, I'll kill you if you dare
   To pose as my competitor.

SOSIA

All this confusion leaves me stupefied;
My reason and my senses are at war.
I've never been so very tired before.
If you'll excuse me, I shall go inside.

MERCURY

Ha! So you wish once more to taste my cane?

SOSIA, *beaten by Mercury*

Oh, no! These heavy blows aren't done in sport;
My back will have to bear a month of pain.
I'll flee this devil, and go back to the port.
Dear gods! My mission was indeed in vain.

MERCURY, *alone*

At last I've driven him off, and made him pay
In drubbings for his many past misdeeds.
But now great Jupiter, who gently leads
The amorous Alcmena, comes this way.

SCENE THREE

JUPITER *(under the form of Amphitryon)*,
ALCMENA, CLEANTHIS, MERCURY

JUPITER

Have the torches, dear Alcmena, remain inside;
I prize their light, which lets me see you clear,
Yet they might give away my presence here,
      Which it is best to hide.

My love, long thwarted through the noble cares
To which I have been bound by martial duty,
Has stolen a little time from such affairs
      And given it to your beauty.

This offering to your charms, this theft of time,
Might well seem guilty in the public view,
And the sole witness I desire is you,
      Who think the deed no crime.

ALCMENA

I take the greatest pride, Amphitryon,
In the glory you have gained through your successes;
    The brilliant victory you've won
Has warmed my spirit's innermost recesses;
But when I ponder how this just renown
      Keeps me from him I chose to marry,

38

My love for you can make me so contrary
    That I view your honors with a frown,
And quarrel with that edict of the crown
Which made you general of our military.
After a victory, it is sweet to find
That one we love has scaled the heights of glory;
But with such fame, such perils are combined
That soon we dread to hear a sadder story.
How many fears one's soul must undergo
When news of any fray or clash is told!
Nor can one think, when chilled and harrowed so,
    Of any way to be consoled
    For the horror of the threatened blow.
Whatever wreath the hero's brow may wear,
Whatever share one has in that high honor,
Is it worth the pains a loving wife must bear
When fears for him at all times weigh upon her?

JUPITER

There's nothing in you that I don't adore;
To deepest love your least look testifies;
And, I must own, it makes my spirit soar
To see such ardor in my dear one's eyes.
But in the affection I receive from you
There's one small thing that troubles me a bit;
It would be even sweeter if I knew
That duty did not enter into it;
That the soft looks and favors that you show me
Stemmed from your passion and my self alone,
And were not tributes to a husband, shown
    Because they're something that you owe me.

[*Act One • Scene Three*]

It's because you are my spouse that my devotion
    Has any right to be expressed;
I don't quite understand this sudden notion
    That's making trouble in your breast.

JUPITER

The love I feel for you—the tenderness—
    No husband could be capable of;
And in our rapturous moments you cannot guess
    The delicacy of my love.
You can't know how a sensitive heart like mine
Dwells upon trifles with devout excess,
    And studies ever to refine
    The manner of its happiness.
    Alcmena dearest, in me you see
A husband, and a lover; and the latter's
The only one, I think, who really matters.
The husband merely cramps and hinders me.
The lover, fiercely jealous of your heart,
Would be the only one for whom you care,
    And will not settle for some part
    Of what the husband deigns to share.
He would obtain your love at its pure source,
And not by way of nuptial bonds and rights,
Or duty, which compels the heart by force
And so corrupts all loving intercourse
    And spoils all amorous delights.
In this small matter which perturbs him so,
He asks that, in your thinking, you divide
Him from that other self he can't abide;

40

That the husband be for virtue and for show
Alone; and that your gracious heart bestow
All love, all passion, on the lover's side.

ALCMENA

Really, Amphitryon,
You must be jesting in this speech you've made;
If anyone overheard you, I'm afraid
      He'd think your wits were gone.

JUPITER

There's much more sense in what I say
    Than you suppose, Alcmena dear.
But I must not prolong my secret stay,
And my departure for the port draws near.
Farewell. Harsh duty says our tryst is over,
      And tears me from you for a space.
Fair one, when next you see your husband's face,
      Think too, I pray you, of the lover.

ALCMENA

What the gods have joined, I shall not separate;
For husband and lover both, my love is great.

CLEANTHIS, *aside*

Oh, my! How sweet is the caress
Of a spouse on whom one's heart can dote!
And my wretched husband—how remote
He is from all such tenderness!

41

[*Act One • Scene Three*]

MERCURY, *aside*

I shall go tell the goddess Night
That it's time she furled her shades and fled;
The sun must rise now from his bed,
And sweep the litter of the stars from sight.

SCENE FOUR

CLEANTHIS, MERCURY

CLEANTHIS, *halting Mercury, who was departing*

How can you leave me in that way?

MERCURY

What ails you, woman? I propose
To do my duty as valet,
And follow where my lord Amphitryon goes.

CLEANTHIS

But must you part from me, you lout,
In a manner so abrupt and rough?

MERCURY

That's a strange thing to complain about.
God knows we'll be together long enough!

CLEANTHIS

So! You take leave of me in brutal style,
Without one loving word or tender smile!

MERCURY

How in the devil should I still know
What pretty words to please you by?
In fifteen years of marriage, talk runs dry.
We've said our say to each other, long ago.

CLEANTHIS

Look at Amphitryon, you beast;
See how his ardor for his wife is shown;
And blush then, since you fail to make the least
Display of feeling toward your own.

MERCURY

Heavens, Cleanthis, they're at the amorous age;
After a time, all that will pass;
What now becomes them, at this early stage,
Would, in old married folk like us, seem crass;
How would it be to see us two engage
In sugary talk, like lad and lass?

CLEANTHIS

Wretch! Do you mean that I'm no longer fair,
And could not hope to inspire a sigh?

MERCURY

Oh no, I'd not say that, not I;
But I'm too old for sighing—I wouldn't dare,
And I'd be laughed at should I try.

44

[*Act One • Scene Four*]

CLEANTHIS

Do you deserve—you, with your squalid life—
To have a virtuous woman as your wife?

MERCURY

Great gods! You're virtuous to excess,
And your goodness does me little good.
Stop playing Spotless Womanhood
And badger me a little less.

CLEANTHIS

You talk as if my virtue were a sin!

MERCURY

Sweetness is woman's most endearing trait;
Your virtue makes a ceaseless din,
And keeps me in a frazzled state.

CLEANTHIS

Would you prefer the feigning tenderness
Of the sort of wife who, full of pretty talents,
Smothers her spouse with kiss and warm caress,
To make him overlook her many gallants?

MERCURY

Do you want a frank reply from me?
What's cuckoldry? Only fools are troubled by it.
From now on, let my motto be
"Less honor, and more peace and quiet."

[*Act One • Scene Four*]

CLEANTHIS

Do you mean to say that you simply wouldn't care
If I and some gallant had a love affair?

MERCURY

Not if it cured you of the need to scold,
And caused your shrewish temper to desert you.
    An easygoing vice, I hold,
    Is better than an angry virtue.
    Farewell, Cleanthis, my duck, my lamb.
    I must attend Amphitryon.

CLEANTHIS, *alone*

    If in my heart there were one dram
Of courage, I'd make him pay for all he's done.
    Oh, but I feel a simpleton
    To be the honest wife I am!

ACT TWO

SCENE ONE

AMPHITRYON, SOSIA

AMPHITRYON

Come here, you knave. Come here, you parasite.
Your words would justify my thrashing you,
And, if I had a stick, I soon would do
    What all these saucy lies invite.

SOSIA

Sir, if you see things in that light,
I've nothing more to say; I'm through;
And you shall be always in the right.

AMPHITRYON

Wretch, would you have me trust in tales that were
Clearly no more than foolish fantasies?

SOSIA

No. I'm the servant and you're the master, Sir;
The truth shall be exactly what you please.

[*Act Two • Scene One*]

AMPHITRYON

Well, I'll put down my anger. I wish to hear
About your mission, and all its incidents.
　　Before I see my wife, a clear
Picture is needed of these late events.
Collect your wits, then; make your thoughts cohere,
And answer me with point and pertinence.

SOSIA

　　But, lest I somehow miss my cue,
　　Tell me, I pray, before we start,
In what way you would have me answer you.
Shall I speak, Sir, from my conscience and my heart,
Or as the hangers-on of great folk do?
　　Shall what I say be simply true,
　　Or shall I speak with flattering art?

AMPHITRYON

　　No, it's your only obligation
To give an account that's truthful and sincere.

SOSIA

Good. I'll comply, Sir, never fear.
Proceed with your interrogation.

AMPHITRYON

When I gave you a certain order yesterday? . . .

[*Act Two • Scene One*]

SOSIA

I set out under skies both black and bleak,
Cursing you as I made my painful way,
And railing at the order of which you speak.

AMPHITRYON

What, rascal!

SOSIA

Sir, if it's not the truth you seek,
Just bid me lie, and I'll obey.

AMPHITRYON

Behold with what goodwill our lackeys serve us!
No matter. And on the journey, what occurred?

SOSIA

I was made gibberingly nervous
By the least thing that peeped or stirred.

AMPHITRYON

You coward!

SOSIA

Nature, in forming us, contrives
To give us temperaments which greatly vary;
Some revel in finding ways to risk their lives:
I, in avoiding all that's scary.

51

[*Act Two • Scene One*]

AMPHITRYON

When you reached the house? . . .

SOSIA

I thought that for a while
I might rehearse my lines, outside the door,
Deciding in what tone and style
To speak my glorious tidings of the war.

AMPHITRYON

And then?

SOSIA

Then someone came and cut me short.

AMPHITRYON

Who?

SOSIA

Sosia; another me; a man who was
Dispatched by you to Alcmena from the port,
And who knows our secrets, of whatever sort,
As well as the me now speaking does.

AMPHITRYON

What rubbish!

[*Act Two* • *Scene One*]

SOSIA

Those are the facts, Sir, of the case.
That me was at the house ahead of me;
    For I had got there, don't you see,
    Before I ever reached the place.

AMPHITRYON

    Pray, where in the devil did you find
    Such nonsense? Have you lost your mind?
    To what else could this be assigned—
    To drink, or dreams, or both combined?
    Or humor of a sickly kind?

SOSIA

    No, Sir, it's simply what occurred;
    There's nothing frivolous about it.
I'm a man of honor, and you have my word;
    I tell you, though you're free to doubt it,
That, thinking myself one Sosia, I drew near
    Our gate, and found that I was two;
That, of the rival me's who parleyed here,
One's now in the house, while the other talks with you;
That the me you see, road-weary and half dead,
Found the other chipper, fresh, and wide awake,
    Without a worry in his head
    Save how to find some bones to break.

AMPHITRYON

    My nature must be, I surmise,
Patient, and calm, and gentle to the core,
If I let a lackey feed me all these lies!

SOSIA

Careful; don't lose your temper, or
I shall not tell you any more.
We so agreed, you realize.

AMPHITRYON

Well, I'll restrain myself and hear you out,
As promised. But tell me honestly, if you would:
Does this weird mystery you've told about
    Have the least shadow of likelihood?

SOSIA

No, you're quite right. What I've described must seem
    Beyond belief, I must confess.
    What it all means, one cannot guess.
It's a stupid tale, ridiculous and extreme,
    Which shocks one's reason like a dream;
    But it's a fact, Sir, nonetheless.

AMPHITRYON

What must one do to believe it—go insane?

SOSIA

I too was doubtful, and inclined to take
My doubleness as a sign of mental strain;
I thought my other self a fraud, a fake;
But at last he made me see that I was twain;
I saw that he was I, and no mistake;
From head to foot he's like me—handsome, clever,
Well-made, with charms no lady could withstand;
    In short, two drops of milk were never
    So much alike as we are, and,

54

But for a certain heaviness in his hand,
    I'd see no difference whatever.

AMPHITRYON

Oh, this takes patience and self-discipline!
But tell me, now; did you not go inside?

SOSIA

    Ha! Go inside, despite my twin?
Am I so reckless? Am I a suicide?
Did I not bar myself from going in?

AMPHITRYON

How?

SOSIA

    With a stick, which thumped my hide
So fiercely, that my back still hurts like sin.

AMPHITRYON

You were beaten?

SOSIA

Indeed.

AMPHITRYON

By whom?

SOSIA

By me.

AMPHITRYON

By you?

SOSIA

Yes; not the me you're talking to,
But the one inside, who wields a wicked paddle.

AMPHITRYON

May Heaven confound you for this fiddle-faddle!

SOSIA

My words were serious and correct.
The me whom I have met of late
Excels the me you see, in one respect;
His arm is strong, his courage great;
Of these I've felt the full effect;
The me to whom I owe my battered state
Is a fiend whose furies are unchecked.

AMPHITRYON

Well, on with it. You've seen my wife?

SOSIA

No.

[*Act Two • Scene One*]

AMPHITRYON

Why?

SOSIA

For reasons that I've given before.

AMPHITRYON

Explain, you scoundrel. What were you hindered by?

SOSIA

Must I say the same thing twenty times and more?
It was that me who's more robust than I;
That me who wouldn't let me in the door;
    That me who fed me humble pie;
    Who wants to be the only me,
    And looks on me with jealous eye;
    That me whose rage could terrify
My craven self, and make me flee;
That me who's in our house nearby;
That me who smote me hip and thigh
Till I confessed his mastery.

AMPHITRYON

He drank too much last night, I judge, and must
    Be still quite muddled in the head.

SOSIA

If I drank a thing but water, strike me dead!
    I give my oath, which you should trust.

[Act Two • Scene One]

AMPHITRYON

It must be, then, that sleep benumbed your sense,
And that a dream, all full of strange confusions,
   Caused you to have these wild delusions
   Which you describe as real events.

SOSIA

That's not true either. I didn't sleep last night,
   Which I still don't feel inclined to do.
   I'm wide awake as I talk to you;
This morning I was wide awake, all right,
And the other Sosia was conscious, too,
   As he battered me with all his might.

AMPHITRYON

   Follow me, now, and do be still.
   My mind's been wearied quite enough.
I am an ass to let a servant fill
My patient ear with all this foolish stuff.

SOSIA, *aside*

   All speech is foolish if it's framed
   By someone of obscure estate:
   But the same words, uttered by the great,
   Would be applauded and acclaimed.

[*Act Two • Scene One*]

Let's enter, without more delays.
But look, my fair Alcmena is coming out;
She doesn't expect me yet, and so, no doubt,
    She'll be surprised to see my face.

SCENE TWO

ALCMENA, *not seeing Amphitryon*

Cleanthis, let us approach the gods, and do
    Them homage in my husband's name,
Thanking them for the victory which through
His valorous deeds, the Theban state can claim.
           (Seeing Amphitryon:)
Oh!

AMPHITRYON

    May victorious Amphitryon
Be welcomed by his loving wife anew!
May Heaven, which restores you to my view,
Restore as well the peerless heart I won,
    And may that heart look fondly on
    Your spouse, as he now looks on you!

ALCMENA

What! Back so soon?

AMPHITRYON

        Those words, I'm forced to say,
Don't welcome me in very ardent fashion.

60

On such occasions as today,
To say "What! Back so soon?" is not the way
　　To manifest a burning passion.
　　I dared suppose that in this case
You'd feared for me, and missed me; was I wrong?
Yearning for someone, when desire is strong,
Makes every moment move at sluggish pace,
　　And the absence of a cherished face,
However brief, is always far too long.

ALCMENA

I don't see . . .

AMPHITRYON

　　　　No, Alcmena; when thoughts are on
An absent love, the minutes seem to crawl;
　　But you've reckoned the time that I've been gone
　　Like one who doesn't love at all.
　　When we are truly amorous,
The briefest parting is an agony,
　　And the one whom we delight to see
　　Cannot come back too soon for us.
　　My fervent feelings, I confess,
Were disappointed by your words of greeting;
　　I thought your heart, at such a meeting,
Would melt, instead, with joy and tenderness.

ALCMENA

　　I can't imagine what could be
The basis of that speech just uttered bỳ you;
　　And if you have complaints of me
　　I don't know, in all honesty,

61

What I could do to satisfy you.
Last night, when you so happily returned,
I was, I think, most joyous and most tender,
    Answering the love with which you burned
With all the love a woman's heart could render.

AMPHITRYON

What? What?

ALCMENA

    Did I not plainly manifest
My rapturous delight? Did I not clearly
Convey to you how glad I felt, how blest,
To see once more a spouse I loved so dearly?

AMPHITRYON

What are you saying?

ALCMENA

    That you showed no lack
Of joy, yourself, when I thus rhapsodized;
And that, since you departed at the crack
Of dawn, and then so suddenly came back,
    I had some right to be surprised.

AMPHITRYON

Perhaps, Alcmena, you anticipated,
Last night, in visions of your sleeping mind,
    The glad return I contemplated,
And having, in this dream your mind created,

Repaid my eager love in kind,
Feel that your heart is vindicated?

ALCMENA

Perhaps, Amphitryon, you are aberrated,
    And vapors so becloud your mind
That memories of last night are dissipated,
And you can question all that I have stated,
    And my true love, by your unkind
Mistrust, be slandered and negated?

AMPHITRYON

Those vapors that you've given me seem,
To say the least, a little strange.

ALCMENA

I think that they're a fair exchange
For that imaginary dream.

AMPHITRYON

Unless you had a dream, there is no way
The things you've said to me can be excused.

ALCMENA

Unless those vapors make your head confused,
One cannot justify the things you say.

AMPHITRYON

Enough of vapors, Alcmena; you've had your sport.

63

ALCMENA

Enough too of that dream, Amphitryon.

AMPHITRYON

A joke can soon be overdone,
When it concerns a matter of this sort.

ALCMENA

Yes; and to lend those words support,
I feel a slight impatience coming on.

AMPHITRYON

Is this how you will make it up to me
For the cold welcome of which I have complained?

ALCMENA

Is this amnesia that you've feigned
Amusing you sufficiently?

AMPHITRYON

Oh, Heavens, Alcmena, let's stop right where we are,
And talk a little sense.

ALCMENA

Amphitryon, don't go on with this pretense;
You've carried the joke too far.

AMPHITRYON

Come, will you tell me to my face that I
Was here before this present hour, pray?

ALCMENA

Come, shall you have the boldness to deny
That you came here, just at twilight, yesterday?

AMPHITRYON

I came here yesterday?

ALCMENA

           Yes; and left once more
When the first fires of sunrise blazed.

AMPHITRYON, *aside*

Was such a squabble ever heard before?
And would not any hearer be amazed?
Eh, Sosia?

SOSIA

        She needs six grains of hellebore;
I fear, Sir, that her wits are crazed.

AMPHITRYON

Alcmena, by all the gods on high,
Wild talk can have dire consequences!

[*Act Two • Scene Two*]

Before you speak again, do try
To think, and to regain your senses.

ALCMENA

I'm quite sane, and quite serious;
And my whole staff knows you slept beneath this roof.
I don't know why you are behaving thus,
But if there truly were a need for proof
Of what your memory could not restore,
From whom could I have gained, unless from you,
    The news that you had won the war,
And the five diamonds that Pterelas bore
    Until your sword consigned him to
    The shades below for evermore?
How could one ask for surer proofs than those?

AMPHITRYON

I've already given you, you declare,
The cluster of bright diamonds that I chose,
    And which I meant that you should wear?

ALCMENA

Indeed, yes; and of that I'll give you plain,
Convincing evidence.

AMPHITRYON

How?

ALCMENA, *pointing to the diamond cluster on her girdle*

Is *this* not clear?

[*Act Two • Scene Two*]

AMPHITRYON

Sosia!

SOSIA, *taking a jewel box from his pocket*

She's joking, Sir, and I have it here.
That trick of hers will be in vain.

AMPHITRYON, *looking at the jewel box*

The seal's unbroken.

ALCMENA, *placing the diamonds in Amphitryon's hand*

Is this, then, an illusion?
Here. Don't you think that proof is rather strong?

AMPHITRYON

Good gods!

ALCMENA

Amphitryon, no more feigned confusion;
Your silly prank has gone on much too long,
And all things point, you'll grant, to one conclusion.

AMPHITRYON

Quick, break the seal.

[*Act Two • Scene Two*]

SOSIA, *having opened the jewel box*

My word, there's nothing there!
Some witchcraft must have whisked it from its place,
Or else it flew, of its own self, through the air,
    Toward her whose beauty it was meant to grace.

AMPHITRYON, *aside*

O Gods, who guide all creatures everywhere,
What does this thing foretell? What do I face
    That my heart will not find hard to bear?

SOSIA, *to Amphitryon*

If she speaks the truth, we have the selfsame fate,
And just like me, Sir, you'll find that you've been
        doubled.

AMPHITRYON

Hush.

ALCMENA

Why is your surprise so great,
And why do you seem so greatly troubled?

AMPHITRYON, *aside*

Oh, what disorder's in my brain!
I see things with no rational foundation,
And my honor cringes from a revelation
    Which common sense cannot explain.

[*Act Two • Scene Two*]

ALCMENA

With such firm evidence in hand, d'you still
Think to deny your visit here last night?

AMPHITRYON

No; but describe what happened, if you will,
    During this visit that you cite.

ALCMENA

Since you ask me to describe it, do you imply
That the person who came last evening wasn't you?

AMPHITRYON

Forgive me; there's a certain reason why
I need to interrogate you as I do.

ALCMENA

Have the great affairs which occupy your mind
Made you forget last night so very fast?

AMPHITRYON

Perhaps; but now, if you will be so kind,
    Tell me the facts, from first to last.

ALCMENA

The tale's not long. I hastened forth to meet you,
    Full of a pleasurable surprise,
    Held out my longing arms to greet you,
And showed my joy by many happy cries.

AMPHITRYON, *aside*

Ah! That sweet welcome galls my jealousy.

ALCMENA

You gave me that rich present, for a start,
Which from the spoils of war you'd picked for me.
        And then with vehemence and art
You told me all the passion of your heart
(Which martial cares had held in slavery),
Your present joy, the pains of being apart,
And how the thought of me had made you smart
        With fierce impatience to be free;
Oh, never had I known you to impart
Your love in such a sweet, impassioned key.

AMPHITRYON, *aside*

Could a man be put to death more painfully?

ALCMENA

All of those transports, all that tenderness,
As you may imagine, gave me no chagrin;
        Indeed, as you may safely guess,
My heart, Amphitryon, found great charm therein.

AMPHITRYON

And then?

ALCMENA

        We talked; and each would interrupt
The other, to leave no fond concern unsaid.

70

Supper was served and, all alone, we supped;
And after that, we two retired to bed.

AMPHITRYON

Together?

ALCMENA

Of course. That question is absurd.

AMPHITRYON, *aside*

Ah, there's the cruelest blow of all. It's true!
I shook with jealous dread until I knew.

ALCMENA

What made you blush so deeply at that word?
Did I do wrong in going to bed with you?

AMPHITRYON

To my great grief, Alcmena, it was not I;
And whoever says I came here yesterday
    Tells, of all false things one could say,
    The most abominable lie.

ALCMENA

Amphitryon!

AMPHITRYON

Faithless woman!

71

[*Act Two • Scene Two*]

ALCMENA

You've lost your head!

AMPHITRYON

No, no, all gentle talk I now disown:
By grief, my self-control is overthrown,
And in this furious hour my heart is dead
    To all but cold revenge alone.

ALCMENA

Revenge on whom? And if you condemn me so,
    What want of faith it shows in you!

AMPHITRYON

    It wasn't I, that's all I know;
And in my rage, there's nought I might not do!

ALCMENA

Unworthy husband, my facts speak plain and true,
    But your false claims are cruel and low.
    You have no right to assail me thus,
And charge me with unfaithfulness beside.
If you seek, by making this demented fuss,
An excuse to break the bonds with which I'm tied
    To you in wedlock, as your bride,
    Then all this is superfluous:
    For I'm determined, on my side,
This day to loose the chains uniting us.

AMPHITRYON

After the shameful wrong I've now detected,
That's surely a step for which you must prepare:
It is, indeed, the least that can be expected,
  And things perhaps will not rest there.
Dishonor is certain; that I'm betrayed is plain;
Affection cannot veil that from my eye;
But some details of the matter still remain
Which my just wrath intends to clarify.
Your brother can establish, beyond dispute,
That I didn't leave him till this morning's light;
I'm going to fetch him, so that he may refute
Your false assertion that I was here last night.
And then we'll get to the bottom of this case—
  This strange, unheard-of, dark affair;
And when my righteous anger scents the trace,
  Let him who's done me wrong beware!

SOSIA

Sir . . .

AMPHITRYON

  No, you needn't accompany me;
Wait, Sosia, till I come back.

CLEANTHIS, *to Alcmena*

Shall I . . .

ALCMENA

  No, there's nothing that I lack;
Don't follow me, Cleanthis. Let me be.

SCENE THREE

CLEANTHIS, SOSIA

CLEANTHIS, *aside*

His brain, it seems, is in a jangled state;
 But her brother soon will calm his huff
 And put an end to this debate.

SOSIA, *aside*

For my poor master, this blow was hard enough—
 A very painful turn of fate.
I may face revelations just as rough,
And I'd better clear things up, now, with my mate.

CLEANTHIS, *aside*

Let's see if he'll dare to speak to me, the lout!
But no, I mustn't let my feelings show.

SOSIA, *aside*

Things can be disagreeable to know,
 And I tremble at what I might find out.
Perhaps it's safer not to enquire about
 A matter which might cause me woe?
 But I must risk it, and be bold,
 For I just can't keep from wondering.

74

It's an urge that cannot be controlled,
   One's itch to learn the very thing
   That one had rather not be told.
Blessings, Cleanthis!

CLEANTHIS

So, you have the gall
   To face me again, you scoundrel, you!

SOSIA

Lord, what's the matter? You're always in a stew,
   And you take offense at nothing at all!

CLEANTHIS

What do you mean by "nothing"?

SOSIA

What that word
Has always meant in verse, and prose, and such.
   "Nothing," as you have surely heard,
   Means nothing, or at least not much.

CLEANTHIS

What holds me back I do not know,
   You wretch, from scratching out your eyes,
To show how far a woman's wrath can go.

SOSIA

I say! From what did this wild rage arise?

[*Act Two • Scene Three*]

CLEANTHIS

You call it "nothing," then, the brutish way
  In which you treated me of late?

SOSIA

What?

CLEANTHIS

      Ha! You're playing innocent, eh?
  Will you imitate your master, and state
That you truly didn't return here yesterday?

SOSIA

Oh no, for that would be untrue;
  Let me be altogether frank:
We'd had some wine, of which I freely drank,
And it's made me forget whatever it made me do.

CLEANTHIS

What a sly excuse, to claim that you forget—

SOSIA

No, it's the truth, I swear, I vow.
In my condition, I fear I may have let
    Myself do things I should regret,
    And which I can't remember now.

[*Act Two • Scene Three*]

CLEANTHIS

You don't remember how, in act and word,
You treated me, when you came here from the port?

SOSIA

No, tell me my misdeeds, of every sort.
    I'm a just man, and if I've erred,
I'll stand condemned before my own soul's court.

CLEANTHIS

Well, then. Amphitryon said you soon were due,
And I sat up waiting until you should appear;
You came, but you were chilly and severe,
As if I were not anyone you knew.
    And when I sought a kiss from you,
You turned your head and offered me your ear.

SOSIA

Good!

CLEANTHIS

    Good, you say!

SOSIA

               Oh, Heavens, my dear bride,
    Let me explain that, for I can.
I'd eaten garlic, and like a decent man
I turned my breath a little to one side.

77

CLEANTHIS

I expressed to you a tender, wifely love,
But to all I said, you were as cold as stone;
    And you never spoke one syllable of
    Affection, in answer to my own.

SOSIA, *aside*

Courage!

CLEANTHIS

    Despite these loving overtures,
My chaste desires were baffled, as I said;
And so extreme was that cold mood of yours,
That you wouldn't even join me in our bed,
As the law of marriage solemnly adjures.

SOSIA

What! I didn't go to bed?

CLEANTHIS

No.

SOSIA

Can it be true?

CLEANTHIS

    Yes, traitor, it's a certainty.
You gave me the worst affront a spouse could do.
And this morning, was there any apology?

78

No, and you then took leave of me
With words of scorn instead of a fond adieu.

SOSIA

Well done, Sosia!

CLEANTHIS

So that is your reaction!
You laugh, then, at your gross offense!

SOSIA

I feel profound self-satisfaction.

CLEANTHIS

Is that how you express your penitence?

SOSIA

I never dreamt that I had such good sense.

CLEANTHIS

You don't condemn your cold and faithless action,
But burst, instead, with joyous impudence!

SOSIA

Hold on! If I seem joyous to your eyes,
It's because my heart delights in doing right;
Instinctively, I did what was most wise,
In acting toward you as I did last night.

79

CLEANTHIS

You scoundrel! Are you making fun?

SOSIA

No, all I say may be believed.
I felt a certain apprehension—one
Which, after you had spoken, was relieved.
I was in terror, fearing that we'd done
A deed for which we later might have grieved.

CLEANTHIS

What dreadful deed did you so wisely shun?

SOSIA

When a man is drunk, the doctors hold,
Lovemaking ought to be eschewed,
Since children so conceived are always rude
And sickly, and the black sheep of the fold.
What if my mood, last night, had not been cold?
Think of what sad results might have ensued!

CLEANTHIS

I wish all doctors were in Hell;
Their theories are lunatic.
Let them give orders to the sick,
And not prescribe for people who are well.
They meddle too much in our affairs,
Giving our chaste desires harsh rules to follow;
And when the dog days come, their wares

Are just the same—those grim decrees of theirs,
   And a lot of old wives' tales to swallow.

SOSIA

Gently, now.

CLEANTHIS

      No, such folly I won't approve;
'Twas crackbrained people who conceived those rules.
No wine or weather can blight the doing of
Those duties which belong to married love.
      Your doctors are a pack of fools.

SOSIA

I wish your rage at them would moderate;
They're decent men, whatever the world may say.

CLEANTHIS

In vain you try to appease and palliate:
Your lame excuse won't do, in any way;
And, sooner or later, I'll retaliate
For the cold contempt you show me every day.
I've not forgotten what you said of late,
And I mean to profit, my perfidious mate,
From your most kind permission to go astray.

SOSIA

What?

81

[*Act Two • Scene Three*]

CLEANTHIS

Wretch, you told me that you wouldn't mind
If I took a lover, that I was free—

SOSIA

Oh, no! On second thoughts, I find
That I'd rather you didn't. It would reflect on me.
I urge you to do nothing of the kind.

CLEANTHIS

Still, if I find I can persuade
Myself to do as you suggest . . .

SOSIA

We must break off now, I'm afraid.
Here comes Amphitryon, looking self-possessed.

SCENE FOUR

JUPITER, CLEANTHIS, SOSIA

JUPITER, *aside*

I'll take this opportunity to appease
Alcmena, and to banish her vexation,
And in so doing taste the ecstasies
    Of happy reconciliation.
        (*To Cleanthis:*)
Alcmena is upstairs, I presume?

CLEANTHIS

Yes, in her agitated mood
    She feels a wish for solitude,
And bade me not to follow her to her room.

JUPITER

Whomever else she may have banished,
Her words do not apply to me.

CLEANTHIS

His grief, so far as I can see,
Has, in a matter of minutes, vanished.

SCENE FIVE

CLEANTHIS, SOSIA

SOSIA

What do you think of my master's cheerful mien,
    Cleanthis, after that dreadful brawl?

CLEANTHIS

    Women, I think, should vent their spleen
By sending men to the Devil, one and all;
    The best of them's not worth a bean.

SOSIA

    That's what your anger makes you say;
But women are too attached to men for that;
You'd find existence very drab and flat
    If the Devil took us all away.

CLEANTHIS

You think so, do you?

SOSIA

Hush; it's they.

SCENE SIX

JUPITER, ALCMENA, CLEANTHIS, SOSIA

JUPITER

Fairest Alcmena, do not go!
My heart could not survive that pain.

ALCMENA

No, I can't possibly remain
With you, the author of my woe.

JUPITER

I beg you . . .

ALCMENA

Leave me.

JUPITER

What!

ALCMENA

I tell you, leave me.

85

[*Act Two • Scene Six*]

JUPITER, *sotto voce*, *aside*

Her young tears touch my heart; her sufferings
grieve me.
(*Aloud:*)
Let me at least . . .

ALCMENA

No, no, don't follow me.

JUPITER

Where do you mean to go?

ALCMENA

Where you won't be.

JUPITER

That will be very hard to do.
I am so bound to you, who are so fair,
That not for a moment shall we part, I swear.
Wherever you go, I'll follow you.

ALCMENA

And I shall flee you everywhere.

JUPITER

I must indeed be terrifying!

ALCMENA

You *are* so; more than can be said.
Yes, I behold in you a petrifying
    Monster, a monster dire and dread,
    A monster whose approaching tread
    Frightens its victim into flying.
At the sight of you, my heart is turned to lead;
    I agonize, and feel like dying;
    All of the horrors that bespread
    The earth, and must be feared and fled,
Are less malign than you, less horrifying.

JUPITER

To hear you talk, you hate me rather a lot.

ALCMENA

My heart has still more rage on call,
And it annoys my heart that it cannot
    Find words in which to express it all.

JUPITER

Alcmena, how do I deserve
To be called a monster, and to be chided thus?

ALCMENA

What a thing to ask! How disingenous!
You madden me with your outrageous nerve.

[*Act Two • Scene Six*]

JUPITER

Relent, and let me speak, I pray . . .

ALCMENA

No, never again shall I see or hear you. Never.

JUPITER

Have you the heart to treat me in this way?
    Is this the love that would last forever,
Of which you sweetly spoke just yesterday?

ALCMENA

No, it is not: your brutish nature clashes
    With all that's sweet, and makes it tart.
That tender, passionate love is now but ashes.
You've wantonly destroyed it in my heart
    By a hundred cruel cuts and slashes.
Now, in its place, is a wrath that won't abate,
A bitter scorn that will not dissipate,
A desperate heart, incensed by your affronts,
Which now shall view you with dislike as great
As the love with which it looked upon you once—
    That is to say, with boundless hate.

JUPITER

Your love for me was very weak, perforce,
If by so small a thing it was undone!
Should a little joke occasion a divorce,
And should one bridle at what was meant in fun?

[Act Two • Scene Six]

ALCMENA

Ah, that's what gives me such distress,
And seems unpardonable to me:
The transports of an honest jealousy
        Would trouble me far less.
        Jealousy is a violent notion
Which, like a storm at sea, can rock the soul;
And the wisest spirit, tossed on such an ocean,
        Can find it difficult to control
        The helm of its emotion.
The anger of a heart thus blindly driven
Is someway pardoned, even as it gives offense,
        And can, for all its violence,
Recall the love that gave it birth, and hence
        Make claim to be forgiven.
Yes, he who offends us by a jealous fit
Can always plead its origin in love,
        Which no man is the master of,
        And therefore be absolved of it.
        But, oh, to pass from what was merely
A bit of teasing to a sudden rage;
Without the shadow of a cause, to wage
        War on a heart that loved you dearly,
        And wound my honor so severely;
That was a heartless onslaught which, I fear me,
Nothing will ever soften or assuage.

JUPITER

You're right, Alcmena, as I must concede.
'Twas an odious crime, and I no longer claim
        That there's the least excuse to plead:
But let me exonerate my heart, and name
        The person whom you ought to blame

89

For that unconscionable deed.
Hear me, Alcmena, for this is true:
Only the husband is at fault,
And he should be the culprit, in your view.
The lover had no part in that assault,
And his heart's not capable of slandering you.
That heart, which worships you with humble sighs,
    Would never dream of acting so;
And it would wish, should it in any wise
    Wound you, or cause you any woe,
To be stabbed a hundred times before your eyes.
But the husband's failed to respect you, to maintain
    That deference which you should be shown;
Those harsh words that you heard were his alone,
For he thinks a husband's temper has free rein.
Yes, yes, it's he, the husband, who has transgressed;
It's he who has maltreated you, that's clear.
    He's yours to hate, and to detest;
    I yield him up to you, my dear.
But spare the lover, Alcmena, that severe
    Resentment which is in your breast.
    In this offense, he has no share;
    Detach him from the guilty one,
    And, so as to be just and fair,
Don't punish him for what he hasn't done.

ALCMENA

    The fine distinction that you've made
    Is of a very frivolous kind;
    Such airy nonsense, I'm afraid,
Is not appealing to an angry mind.
In vain you play that silly verbal game.
I'll spare no part of him who does me wrong;
It's the whole man at whom my rage takes aim,

90

And to my anger, just and strong,
The husband and the lover look the same.
Both of them, in my thoughts, combine and fuse;
And both are painted in the same dark hues
    By the heart which they have violated;
Both have insulted me; both I accuse,
    And both, by me, are fiercely hated.

JUPITER

Well then, I'm guilty, as you say,
    So far as this great crime's concerned,
And there is justice in the fiery way
You treat me like some traitor who should be burned.
It's wholly proper that your heart has turned
Against me, and the wrath that you display
Is a harsh torment that I've fully earned.
It's right indeed that you should shun my face,
    And that you threaten ever to
    Elude my steps, if I give chase.
    I must seem wholly vile to you,
And worthy to be skewered through and through.
No deed could be more horrible and base
    Than bringing tears to eyes so blue;
It's a crime against mankind, and Heaven, too;
And I deserve that you should close my case
    By mustering all your hate apace
    To do the worst that it can do.
    Yet I appeal to you for grace,
And go down on my knees to beg it of you,
Pleading with you for mercy in the name
    Of the tenderest and brightest flame
    With which an ardent soul could love you.
    Fairest Alcmena, if you deny

[*Act Two • Scene Six*]

The pardon that I ask, that I implore,
    By one quick thrust, then, shall I die,
    And be delivered from a sore
    And bitter agony which I
    Have not the strength to suffer more.
    Yes, I am in a desperate state,
    Alcmena, and I hope you know
That I, who love your heavenly beauty so,
Could not, for a single day, survive your hate.
Already I feel these minutes, cruel and slow,
    Draining the life of my sad heart,
    Each tick or tock a mortal blow;
A thousand vultures, tearing me apart,
Would hurt far less than what I undergo.
If I've no right to hope for clemency,
Tell me as much, Alcmena, and you shall see
This sword of mine plunge swiftly, to the hilt,
Into a wretched heart that owns its guilt,
A heart that, wronging you, has proven to be
Richly deserving that its blood be spilt.
Yet I'll rejoice in Hades' dark domains
If, by my death, I can appease your ire,
And clear your spirit, as this sad day wanes,
    Of any tinge of hate that stains
    Your memory of my love's pure fire.
That is the one great boon I dare desire.

ALCMENA

Oh, cruel husband!

JUPITER

Speak, speak, and end my pains.

92

[*Act Two • Scene Six*]

ALCMENA

Am I to show you kindness, if you please,
After such insults and indignities?

JUPITER

However much one may abhor his crimes,
Can one reject a lover who repents?

ALCMENA

A proper lover would die a thousand times
Before he gave his loved one any offense.

JUPITER

The more we love, the more we tolerate . . .

ALCMENA

No, speak no further; you deserve my hate.

JUPITER

You hate me, then?

ALCMENA

I do my best; I try;
But all your insults, to my great vexation,
Have not produced the vengeful detestation
I feel I should be driven by.

JUPITER

Why all this struggling and frustration,
When, to avenge you, I'm prepared to die?
Just sentence me to death, and I'll obey you.

ALCMENA

If I can't hate you, how can I wish to slay you?

JUPITER

I cannot live unless the angry feeling
    With which you scald my soul is ended,
And that most gracious pardon is extended
    For which I beg, thus humbly kneeling.
        (*Sosia and Cleanthis also kneel.*)
    Choose, now: I wait in dread to hear
    Whether you'll punish, or forgive.

ALCMENA

    Alas, the one alternative
    That I can choose is all too clear.
My heart's betrayed me utterly, and I'm
    Unable to remain irate:
    If I tell you that I cannot hate,
    Are you not pardoned for your crime?

JUPITER

Ah! Lovely Alcmena, I am overjoyed . . .

[*Act Two • Scene Six*]

ALCMENA

Enough; my weakness makes me much annoyed.

JUPITER

    Go, Sosia; make haste and see,
While this sweet rapture makes my heart expand,
What officers of the army are at hand,
    And bid them come and dine with me.
           (*Sotto voce, aside:*)
    While he is absent for a space,
    Good Mercury shall take his place.

SCENE SEVEN

CLEANTHIS, SOSIA

SOSIA

Our betters know the art of mending fences.
Come, shall we copy them in this,
And have ourselves a little armistice
In which to solve our differences?

CLEANTHIS

You think we can chat our way to wedded bliss?

SOSIA

Then you won't talk?

CLEANTHIS

No.

SOSIA

Oh, well; I don't much care.
The loss is yours.

CLEANTHIS

Come back, you idiot.

SOSIA

No, by the Devil, I shall not,
And it's my turn now to let my temper flare.

CLEANTHIS

Good riddance, then, you beast! So there!
(*Alone:*)
A virtuous woman has a weary lot.

ACT THREE

SCENE ONE

AMPHITRYON

I cannot find her brother anywhere;
My search is vain, my weariness complete.
What could be harsher than the lot I bear?
The man I seek eludes me, yet as my feet
 Lead me distracted here and there,
I meet a throng I have no wish to meet.
A thousand folk I've scarcely seen before,
Unwitting pests, extol our deeds of war,
And madden me with their congratulations.
Tormented as I am by private cares,
I suffer under this applause of theirs,
And their embraces sharpen my impatience.
 Vainly I seek to dodge their dread
 Acclaim, for everywhere I fly,
Their kindly persecution stops me dead;
And as they gush at me, and I reply
 With shrugs and noddings of the head,
I mutter curses at them on the sly.
Ah, me! How little praise and honor mean,
And all else that a brilliant victory brings,
When the soul is overcome with grief so keen!
How gladly one would barter all such things
 If the heart could once more be serene!
 Incessantly, my jealous brain

Dwells on my dark vicissitudes,
    And yet, the more it mulls and broods,
The less it can untangle or explain.
The theft of the diamonds I can understand;
A seal will not deter a clever thief;
But her claim that they were given her by my hand,
Last night, is baffling and beyond belief.
'Twixt men, there can be similarities
Whereby impostors manage to deceive;
But that some crafty rascal could with ease
Impersonate a husband, I can't conceive;
There'd be innumerable disparities
Which any wife would readily perceive.
    As for Thessalian sorcery,
Those famous tales that everybody tells
Of ladies fair seduced through magic spells
Have always seemed preposterous to me;
And it would be a jest of Fate if I,
    Returning from the war in glory,
    Must play the butt of such a story,
    And see my honor lost thereby.
I mean to question her again, and see
If what she said was not a fantasy
Caused by some transient fever of the brain.
    Just Heaven! For my peace of mind,
    Let that be proven; let me find
That she was temporarily insane!

SCENE TWO

MERCURY, *on the balcony of Amphitryon's house,*
unseen and unheard by Amphitryon

Since, here, I've no amours to give me pleasure,
I shall devise some other sport instead,
And put some life into my tedious leisure
By driving poor Amphitryon out of his head.
In a god, that sounds uncharitable and callous,
But it's not my nature to behave benignly;
    My planet's attributes incline me
    To deal in mischief and in malice.

AMPHITRYON

Why has this door been locked so very early?

MERCURY

Ho! Easy there! Who's knocking?

AMPHITRYON, *not seeing Mercury*

I.

103

[*Act Three • Scene Two*]

MERCURY

Who's I?

AMPHITRYON, *perceiving Mercury, whom he takes to be Sosia*

Ah! Open up.

MERCURY

For you? Who *are* you? Why
Must you make so great a noise, and sound so surly?

AMPHITRYON

What! Don't you know me?

MERCURY

No, my lad,
And you're no one I would care to know.

AMPHITRYON, *aside*

Has everyone, today, gone raving mad?
Is folly catching? Sosia! Sosia! Hullo!

MERCURY

Sosia's the name I've always had;
It's good of you to remind me, though.

[*Act Three • Scene Two*]

AMPHITRYON

Do you see me clearly?

MERCURY

          Yes. What makes you wreak
Such battery on the door? My word!
What do you want, eh? What do you seek?

AMPHITRYON

What do I want, you gallows-bird?

MERCURY

What do you *not* want, then? Come, speak,
If you want your wishes to be heard.

AMPHITRYON

Just wait, you wretch! I'll come up there
With a stick, and make my feelings plain,
And teach you what it costs, in pain,
To address me with that saucy air.

MERCURY

Take care! If you lay one knuckle on that door,
I'll send you missives of a hurtful type.

AMPHITRYON

Gods! Was such insolence ever heard before?
And from a lackey, too! A guttersnipe!

105

[*Act Three • Scene Two*]

MERCURY

Well, have you sized me up, and looked your fill?
Have you pierced me with that gaze so fierce and grim?
Look at the great big glaring eyes on him!
    My, my! Already, if looks could kill,
      He would have stared me limb from limb.

AMPHITRYON

I shudder to see you work your own undoing
    By all these rash remarks you make.
Above your head, a terrible storm is brewing!
What a shower of blows your back is going to take!

MERCURY

My friend, unless you say a prompt good-bye,
I'll play a tune upon your skeleton.

AMPHITRYON

If you did, you blackguard, I'd show you what is done
To men who attack their masters. Best not try.

MERCURY

Ha! You, my master!

AMPHITRYON

    Knave, that you can't deny.

MERCURY

I have no master save Amphitryon.

AMPHITRYON

And who is this Amphitryon, if not I?

MERCURY

Amphitryon—you!

AMPHITRYON

Of course.

MERCURY

You're addled, son.
Tell me, in what fine pothouse, or what inn,
Has drinking turned your wits askew?

AMPHITRYON

More gibes!

MERCURY

Was the wine of noble origin?

AMPHITRYON

Good gods!

MERCURY

Was the vintage old, or new?

AMPHITRYON

What gall!

MERCURY

New wine can cause the head to spin,
Unless you add some water, too.

AMPHITRYON

I'm going to tear your tongue out, do you hear?

MERCURY

Now, now, good friend, you'd best move on;
You might disturb someone, I fear.
Wine is a powerful thing. Be off, begone,
And leave Amphitryon to enjoy his dear.

AMPHITRYON

What! Is Amphitryon within?

MERCURY

Oh, yes:
Crowned with victorious laurels, and with his bride,
The fair Alcmena, at his side,
He shares an hour of dulcet happiness.

[*Act Three • Scene Two*]

After a curious sort of lovers' tiff,
They're now recovering their amorous poise.
Take care: don't interrupt their secret joys,
    Unless you'd have him give you a stiff
    Beating for that unwelcome noise.

SCENE THREE

AMPHITRYON

AMPHITRYON

Oh, but he's dealt my soul a staggering blow,
And given my poor mind a brutal jar!
If things are as the rascal says they are,
Look how my love and honor are brought low!
Whether to hush things up, or to proclaim
    This outrage, reason must decide.
Should I speak out in anger, or should I hide
    This blot upon my house and name?
But need I *think*, when the wrong is so extreme?
What matter if I publish or conceal?
    Let bitter hate be all I feel,
    And vengeance be my only theme.

SCENE FOUR

AMPHITRYON *and* SOSIA; NAUCRATES *and* POLIDAS
at the back of the stage

SOSIA, *to Amphitryon*

Sir, I've done my best, but the best that I could do
Was to bring you those two gentlemen whom you see.

AMPHITRYON

So you're here, eh?

SOSIA

Sir.

AMPHITRYON

You insolent vermin, you!

SOSIA

What's this?

AMPHITRYON

I'll teach you to make game of me.

111

[*Act Three • Scene Four*]

SOSIA

What's the matter?

AMPHITRYON, *drawing his sword*

"What's the matter," eh? You cur!

SOSIA, *to Naucrates and Polidas*

Please help me, gentlemen! Quickly! Come!

NAUCRATES, *to Amphitryon*

I pray you, hold.

SOSIA

Of what am I guilty, Sir?

AMPHITRYON

No need to tell you that, you scum!
    (*To Naucrates, who is restraining him:*)
My just wrath has a right to be expressed.

SOSIA

When they hang a fellow, at least they tell him why.

NAUCRATES, *to Amphitryon*

Do tell us in what way this man's transgressed.

SOSIA

Yes, gentlemen, press him to reply.

AMPHITRYON

Just now he had the cheek—d'you hear?—
To shut my own door in my face;
And then, with many a threat and jeer,
He sought to run me off the place.
         (*Seeking to strike Sosia:*)
You scoundrel, you!

SOSIA, *dropping to his knees*

I'm dead.

NAUCRATES, *to Amphitryon*

Be calm, I pray.

SOSIA

Gentlemen!

POLIDAS, *to Sosia*

Yes?

SOSIA

Have I been beaten yet?

AMPHITRYON, *to Naucrates*

No, I insist that he must pay
For his impudent words, and that's a heavy debt.

SOSIA

How could I do the things you say,
When I was gathering guests for your little fête?
These gentlemen right here could tell you how
I've just invited them to dine with you.

NAUCRATES

Yes, yes, he brought your message to us just now,
And he never left us. It's all quite true.

AMPHITRYON

Who bade you invite them?

SOSIA

You did, Sir.

AMPHITRYON

When?

SOSIA

After your reconciliation—
When, having soothed Alcmena's deep vexation,
You rejoiced at being one again with her.
(*Sosia stands up again.*)

AMPHITRYON

Great Heavens! At every step I take,
New sufferings are added to my throes,
    And all's so muddled and opaque,
I don't know what to say or to suppose.

NAUCRATES

The happenings at your house, of which he's told,
    Transcend the natural, and ere
You do some deed that's daft or overbold,
You must find out the truth of this affair.

AMPHITRYON

Then let's find out together, you and I;
The Heavens have sent you here most apropos.
Let's see what fortune this day will bestow,
What fate behind these mysteries may lie.
    It is a thing I burn to know,
    And fear more than I fear to die.
        (*Amphitryon knocks at the door of his house.*)

115

SCENE FIVE

JUPITER, AMPHITRYON, NAUCRATES, POLIDAS, SOSIA

JUPITER

Who makes me come downstairs? Who knocks
As if he were the master here?

AMPHITRYON

Gods! What do I see?

NAUCRATES

Oh, what a paradox
That two Amphitryons should at once appear!

AMPHITRYON, *aside*

My heart is utterly congealed:
Alas, I am undone; my quest is ended.
My destiny is now revealed;
One glance, and all is comprehended.

NAUCRATES

The more I scan and scrutinize these two,
The more each man is like the other one.

[*Act Three • Scene Five*]

SOSIA, *crossing to the side of Jupiter*

Sirs, this is the real Amphitryon;
The other's an impostor, through and through.

POLIDAS

Despite minute comparison,
I cannot tell you who is who.

AMPHITRYON

You've all been hoodwinked by a charlatan;
This sword will break the spell that's binding you.

NAUCRATES, *to Amphitryon, who has drawn his sword*

Stop!

AMPHITRYON

No!

NAUCRATES

What dreadful deed would you perform?

AMPHITRYON

I'd punish that impostor's vile deceit.

[*Act Three • Scene Five*]

JUPITER

Gently, now: there's no need to rage and storm;
Men judge, when someone's temper is overwarm,
That an honest cause would not require such heat.

SOSIA

Yes, he's a sorcerer who can take the form
Of any head of household he may meet.

AMPHITRYON, *to Sosia*

For those outrageous words, you knave,
I vow that I shall give you many a stroke.

SOSIA

My master's heart is kind and brave,
And he won't let people beat his serving-folk.

AMPHITRYON

Now let me sate my anger, and in the gore
Of a rank villain wash my shame away.

NAUCRATES, *stopping Amphitryon*

No, we shall not permit so strange a fray—
Amphitryon and himself at war!

AMPHITRYON

What! Will my friends forsake my honor so,
And come to the defense of that low sneak?

118

[*Act Three • Scene Five*]

Gods! Far from furthering the revenge I seek,
They stand between my just wrath and my foe!

NAUCRATES

But how, with any confidence,
    Can we make up our minds, and act,
    When two Amphitryons, in fact,
Keep all our loyal feelings in suspense?
We'd be afraid, if we supported you,
That we'd mistaken your identity.
We see in you the great Amphitryon, he
To whom the thanks of rescued Thebes are due;
But we see the same thing in your rival, too,
And we can't tell who the genuine you might be.
    What we must do is obvious:
By our hands, the impostor must be slain.
But the likeness of you two now baffles us,
    And it would be too hazardous
    To strike before the truth's made plain.
    Let us employ our wits and eyes
To find out who's the impostor, you or he;
Once we have solved that puzzle, there will be
No need to tell us where our duty lies.

JUPITER

Well said. Our strange resemblance justifies
Your having doubts of both of us—him, and me.
I'm far too reasonable to criticize
Your hesitation and uncertainty.
Since the eye can't tell us two apart, it's wise
Not to act rashly. Sirs, we quite agree.
You don't see me becoming fierce and hot,
    You see no drawn sword in my hand;

That's a poor way to unsnarl this Gordian knot,
And I have means more certain and more bland.
    One of us is Amphitryon;
But which is he, you've no idea on earth.
I'll soon clear up that mystery, and have done.
Yes, who I am shall be so well set forth
That even he will grant my name and worth,
And the high lineage that gave me birth,
And have no further wrongs to brood upon.
When I bare the truth to you, my words must fall
Upon the listening ears of Thebes entire;
This matter's of such weight as to require
    Wide audience, and I desire
    To explain things in the sight of all.
Alcmena asks of me that explanation.
Her virtue, sullied by this confrontation,
Asks to be proven pure, and that's my aim.
My love for her makes that an obligation;
And I've invited here a delegation
Of noblest chiefs, to hear me clear her name.
While we await those worthies, come and share
    The pleasures of that board whereto
    Good Sosia invited you,
    And honor me by your presence there.

SOSIA

Gentlemen, I was right; behold the winner.
    Behold the true Amphitryon.
    The true Amphitryon's the one
    Who asks us in and gives us dinner.

[*Act Three • Scene Five*]

AMPHITRYON

What worse humiliation could Fate afford?
I'm forced to listen to the things this base
Deceiver has been saying to my face,
And though his discourse makes my hot blood race,
    My friends won't let me draw my sword!

NAUCRATES, *to Amphitryon*

Do have a little patience. Let's wait and hear
    His statement, which should make it clear
    If any wrath is justified.
    Is he a charlatan? I don't know,
    But, I must say, he sounds as though
    He had some reason on his side.

AMPHITRYON

Go, lukewarm friends, go hear him, and applaud:
I've other friends who have more resolution;
They'll share my detestation of this fraud,
And back me as I seek just retribution.

JUPITER

Well, I'll await their coming, and they can be
    Enlightened by my statement, too.

AMPHITRYON

Mere talk, you wretch, won't make you safe from me;
I'll be avenged, whatever you say or do.

121

[*Act Three • Scene Five*]

JUPITER

To all these insults I have heard
I shall not stoop now to reply;
But wait, and I shall by and by
Confound your anger with a word.

AMPHITRYON

Not Heaven itself could give you sanctuary;
And I'll pursue you to the depths of Hell.

JUPITER

That really won't be necessary;
I shan't flee, as you'll soon see very well.

AMPHITRYON, *aside*

While he's at table, I must quickly go
And find some fighting friends who'll share my wrath,
Then hasten on the homeward path
And slaughter him with thrust and blow.

JUPITER

Don't stand on ceremony, now;
Come, enter, if you'll be so kind.

NAUCRATES

This whole affair, I must avow,
Staggers the senses and the mind.

[*Act Three • Scene Five*]

SOSIA

Enough amazement, sirs; go take your seats,
And feast till dawn in pure beatitude.
                    (*Alone:*)
Now I shall gorge, and get into the mood
        To swap brave tales of martial feats!
        I itch for soups and wines and meats;
        I've never had such a lust for food.

SCENE SIX

MERCURY

Halt! So, you poke your nose in at my door,
    You sniffer-out of food and wine!

SOSIA

Ouch! Not so rough, please!

MERCURY

               So, you're back for more!
    You want me to massage your spine.

SOSIA

Spare me, O brave and generous me;
    Do practice more restraint and measure;
    Good Sosia, let poor Sosia be,
And do not beat yourself with so much pleasure.

MERCURY

From whom did you receive permission
    To use that thrice-forbidden name?

124

[*Act Three • Scene Six*]

Did I not promise to lambaste your frame
If you ignored my stringent prohibition?

SOSIA

Since we serve one master, it's a name that we
        May both, without confusion, share.
I am addressed as Sosia everywhere;
        I gladly allow you to be he;
        Grant me the same; it's only fair.
        Let's let the two Amphitryons
        Have jealous quarrels that never cease,
        And be their own fierce partisans,
While the two Sosias live in perfect peace.

MERCURY

No, one of them's enough; I'll let no other
        Divide my self and name in two.

SOSIA

I'll gladly yield the precedence to you;
I'll be the younger, and you the older brother.

MERCURY

No, a brother is an annoyance I'll forgo;
        I want to be an only son.

SOSIA

        O cruel heart! O tyrannous one!
Permit me at least to be your shadow.

MERCURY

No.

SOSIA

Oh, come; be human; show me some compassion!
Let me, in that dim rôle, be at your side:
I'll shadow you in such obsequious fashion
    That you'll be pleased and gratified.

MERCURY

No quarter; your appeal's denied.
If you dare set foot again on this estate,
    You'll get the usual thousand blows.

SOSIA

Alas, poor Sosia! Your fate
Is very cruel, Heaven knows.

MERCURY

What! Do you still presume to give
Yourself a name I've told you to resign?

SOSIA

The name I mentioned wasn't mine;
That Sosia was a relative
Somewhere in my paternal line,
    Whom someone harsh and primitive
Drove off once, just when it was time to dine.

MERCURY

Well, as for names, if you desire to live,
Learn to distinguish between Mine and Thine.

SOSIA, *aside*

How I'd thrash you, if my courage weren't so weak,
You son of a strumpet, all puffed up with pride!

MERCURY

What?

SOSIA

Nothing.

MERCURY

It seems to me I heard you speak.

SOSIA

Ask anyone; I merely sighed.

MERCURY

Yet someone muttered something about
"Son of a strumpet" in my hearing;
I'm sure of it.

[*Act Three • Scene Six*]

SOSIA

It was, no doubt,
Some parrot, thrilled to see the weather clearing.

MERCURY

Farewell. Remember, if your back should itch,
That this is the place in which I dwell.

SOSIA, *alone*

Ah! Dinnertime's an hour at which
To be excluded is to be in Hell.
But let's accept what the grim Fates have spun;
Let's do what their blind whim would have me do,
And, in a fitting liaison,
Let's join the unfortunate Sosia to
Unfortunate Amphitryon—
Who now, with reinforcements, comes in view.

SCENE SEVEN

AMPHITRYON, ARGATIPHONTIDAS, POSICLES, *and* SOSIA—
the last in a corner of the stage, unseen

AMPHITRYON, *to several other officers who accompany him*

Stop there, gentlemen; keep to my rear a bit,
    And don't advance, I beg of you,
    Until there is a need for it.

POSICLES

I know that this great blow must grieve you sadly.

AMPHITRYON

Yes, all my being is most sorely tried,
    And I suffer in my love as badly
    As in my honor and my pride.

POSICLES

If the likeness is as great as you report,
    Alcmena might not be to blame . . .

AMPHITRYON

    Ah, in a matter of this sort,
Error, though pure, is guilty all the same,

129

And innocence gets no mercy from the court.
Such errors, in whatever light one views them,
    Are bound to touch us where we live,
And though our reason often may excuse them,
Our honor and our love will not forgive.

ARGATIPHONTIDAS

I don't let such ideas confuse my thought;
But I scorn your other friends for their delay;
Such hanging back, I say, is good for nought;
A brave man never would behave that way.
When a friend enlists us in his cause, we ought
    To plunge headfirst into the fray.
Argatiphontidas hates compromise.
For men of honor, it's wrong to listen to
A comrade's foe, and meekly hear his view,
When the voice of vengeance calls for his demise.
    Negotiation I despise:
In a case like this, the first thing one should do
    Is hack the bloody swine in two,
    Rather than talk and temporize.
    Yes, come what may, as you shall see,
Argatiphontidas will perform his task;
    And when we meet your enemy,
    Promise me, Sir—it's all I ask—
That the scoundrel may be killed by me.

AMPHITRYON

Come, then!

SOSIA, *to Amphitryon, clasping his knees*

I kneel, Sir, and await your dread

130

Chastisement of my impudence and nerve.
Bludgeon me, Sir; rain blows upon my head,
   Or in your fury strike me dead:
    'Twill be no more than I deserve,
And not one word of protest shall be said.

AMPHITRYON

Get up. What's happening?

SOSIA

               I've been evicted, too.
I thought to join the rest in festive eating,
    But found that I was there anew
    To offer me a brutal greeting.
Yes, the other me, who serves the other you,
    Has given me another beating.
    Sir, we are similarly fated,
    And similarly victimized.
    Just as I've been dis-Sosiated,
    You have been de-Amphitryonized.

AMPHITRYON

Follow me.

SOSIA

Someone's coming; it's best we waited.

131

SCENE EIGHT

CLEANTHIS, AMPHITRYON, ARGATIPHONTIDAS,
POLIDAS, NAUCRATES, POSICLES, SOSIA

CLEANTHIS

Oh, mercy!

AMPHITRYON

Why this cry of fear?
Why do you look so terrified?

CLEANTHIS

Alas, you're up there, and I see you here!

NAUCRATES, *to Amphitryon*

No hurry; he shortly will appear
And speak, and all this will be clarified.
If one may credit what we heard inside,
Your grief will soon give way to better cheer.

SCENE NINE

MERCURY, AMPHITRYON, ARGATIPHONTIDAS,
POLIDAS, NAUCRATES, CLEANTHIS, SOSIA

MERCURY

Yes, all shall hear him. Prepare to see the great
    Master of all the gods on high,
Who, in the likeness of her cherished mate,
Descended to Alcmena from the sky.
    And as for me, I'm Mercury,
Who gave this rogue, for pastime, many a whack,
    And borrowed his identity;
But now he need not think his fate so black,
    For it's an honor to have one's back
    Lambasted by a deity.

SOSIA

My goodness, Mister God, I thank Your Grace;
But I could have done without your gracious favor.

MERCURY

Let him be Sosia now; he has my waiver;
I'm tired of wearing a mug so commonplace,
And up in Heaven, at my ambrosial laver,
    I'll wash those features off my face.
        (*Mercury flies up to Heaven.*)

[*Act Three • Scene Nine*]

SOSIA

May Heaven keep you away from me forever!
Your malice is implacable and evil.
    Truly, in all my life I've never
    Met any god so like a devil.

SCENE TEN

JUPITER, AMPHITRYON, NAUCRATES, ARGATIPHONTIDAS,
POLIDAS, POSICLES, CLEANTHIS, SOSIA

JUPITER, *announced by the sound of thunder,*
armed with his thunderbolt, in a cloud, on his eagle

Behold, Amphitryon, your impostor; see
How Jove looks when his features are his own.
By these my symbols I am readily known,
And I am sure that this epiphany
    Will free your heart from rage and moan,
And fill your house once more with harmony.
My name, which the world adores at every minute,
Will stifle any scandal that might occur:
    To share a love with Jupiter
    Has surely no dishonor in it;
And surely it must seem a glorious thing
To be the rival of Olympus' king.
You have, I think, no shame or wrong to bear,
    And it is I, in this affair,
Who, god though I am, must utter jealous sighs.
Alcmena's wholly yours, whatever one does,
And it should warm your heart to realize
That the only way for one to please her was
    To assume her cherished husband's guise;
That Jove, revealed in his immortal splendor,
Could not have tempted her to be untrue,

And that her gifts to him of tender
Love were truly given only to you.

SOSIA

Lord Jove knows how to sugarcoat the pill.

JUPITER

Then overcome your dark resentment, please,
And bid your agitated heart be still.
A child shall be born to you, whose fame shall fill
The universe; you shall call him Hercules.
Your future days, replete with all good things,
Will show the world that you are in my care,
    And lesser mortals everywhere
    Will envy what my favor brings.
    You may feel confident about
    The promised joys I adumbrate,
    And which it were a crime to doubt:
    For when the voice of Jove rings out,
    His words are the decrees of Fate.
        (*He vanishes into the clouds.*)

NAUCRATES

These gracious gifts are cause for jubilation . . .

SOSIA

Will you allow me, sirs, a small request?
    Do not embark with too much zest
    On speeches of congratulation:
    Such compliments, let me suggest,

Would seem, to all, embarrassing at best
    In so complex a situation.
We have been honored by the Gods' great King,
Who offers us unparalleled largesse;
Our future is replete with each good thing,
And we shall have, to crown our happiness,
A son with whose renown the world shall ring;
    And all that's very fine, I guess;
    But let us cut our speeches short,
And quietly retire now, if you will.
    Regarding matters of this sort,
    It's wisest always to be still.

AFTERWORD

I was eleven years old when I read
Molière's Amphitryon *to myself for the first time;*
I laughed so hard that I fell over backward.
—VOLTAIRE

Troubled by ill health and by the continuing difficulties of his play *Tartuffe*, a version of which was banned yet again in August, Molière retreated for much of 1667 into a rented house in Auteuil. What came of this retirement was *Amphitryon*, a play very different from his other major comedies. Its characters were not seventeenth-century French people but ancient Greeks and Greek gods with Roman names; its comedy had not the consistent range and tone of, say, *The School for Wives*, but combined the flavors of vaudeville, of fantasy, of high comedy, and even of opera; its medium was not the conventional Alexandrine couplet, but a supple vers libre that could modulate easily between the several planes of *Amphitryon*'s comic action and unite them. This novel offering, made all the more exciting by the use of stage machines for "flying" the actors, was first presented at the Palais-Royal in January 1668 and had at once a striking success.

The story of Amphitryon is an ancient one; both of Homer's epics allude to it, and Hesiod recounts it. Essentially, it amounts to this: that the father of the gods (Jupiter, in Molière's play) grows enamored once again of a mortal woman—in this case Alcmena, the wife of the Theban general Amphitryon; that during her husband's absence in the field, Jupiter descends to earth, takes the form of Amphitryon, and is thus received into Alcmena's bed; and that the result of their union is the demigod Hercules. Molière's chief source for *Amphitryon* was a Latin tragicomedy of the second century B.C., the *Amphitruo* of Plautus, and he was influenced as well by Jean Rotrou's prior French adaptation, *Les Sosies* (1636). It is generally agreed that Molière, though borrowing freely, made all borrowings his own, and that he conferred on all his material, old or new, a decisive unity, humanizing the deities of the tale and telling it entirely in the key of comedy.

The plot and subplot of this play tell how two gods, Jupiter and Mercury, usurp the identities of two mortals, Amphitryon and his valet, Sosia. Because that creates a "situation" not only outrageous but (in modern times) incredible, the story belongs to the category of fantastic farce. Nevertheless, this farce has been found, by many readers and scholars, to embody a number of ponderable themes. One such theme, that of entrapment in one's role, is introduced in the prologue by Night's "old-fashioned" insistence on Olympian decorum, and Mercury's praise of Jove's periodic refusal to "let the jeweled bounds of Heaven confine him." The theme of constraint and convention recurs variously throughout the play, and especially in such a character as Sosia's bitter wife, Cleanthis, who, as she twice complains, is the prisoner of her conventional virtue. The title character himself may perhaps be seen as a prisoner of his precious honor.

A second motif, which invites comparisons between *Amphitryon* and Molière's *Don Juan*, is the high-handed amorality of the powerful, and their indifference to truth. Mercury assures Night in the prologue that morals apply only to "those of low degree," and Sosia, in Act II, Scene 1, makes it plain that the great require lies and flattery, and would have all fact and opinion tailored to their advantage. To the overbearing Amphitryon, Sosia says, "I'm the servant and you're the master, Sir; / The truth shall be exactly what you please." Above all, we observe a lordly amorality in Jupiter, who for the sake of a night's pleasure disrupts the happy marriage of Alcmena and Amphitryon. A French critic argues that since we the audience are privy to Jove's imposture from the beginning, we feel superior to the baffled Amphitryon and enjoy a complicity with the god. That may in some measure or at some moments be true, but seigneurial license is not the ideal of the play, and Jupiter's behavior should make us think, in modern terms, of something like Fitzgerald's "vast carelessness" of the rich.

The warping effect of masters on servants is a third theme, and it is introduced at the outset by Mercury, who, despite his divinity, is Jove's overworked and complaining lackey. Like all lackeys, Mercury has surrendered his individuality and exists to execute the will of another; when he boasts, he boasts of his association with the mighty: "I, who in Heaven and on earth am known/As the famed messenger of Jove's high throne." It may be assumed, I think, that in some of Mercury's malicious treatment of Sosia or Amphitryon, he resembles the man who, having been bawled out at the office, comes home and kicks the dog. But of course it is Sosia (the largest part in the play, and the one played by Molière) in whom the psychic cost of servitude is most fully shown. Intelligent but spineless, he clearly sees and says that his existence as "Amphitryon's man" has meant the loss of true personality and a life of servile dissimulation. Not being his own man, Sosia is incapable of a free loyalty or a mature love; his stunted emotional life comprises a solicitude for his physical self, in the form of gluttony, cowardice, and narcissism; he further compensates himself by daydreaming (as when he imagines himself Alcmena's valued courtier) and by the exercise of an insolent wit.

The three pervasive ideas I have mentioned all have to do with role and status, and so does a fourth one—the problem of identity. Identity does indeed become a problem when one is confronted with a living, breathing double, and Amphitryon and Sosia respond to the challenge very differently. Amphitryon sees himself as the world sees him—as an honored military hero and the husband of Alcmena. There is an absolute equation, in his mind, between himself and that image, and anyone else who pretends to it must be an impostor deserving of death. Sosia's response is less simple, because in becoming Amphitryon's mere instrument, and a "performer" in both senses of the word, he has already been estranged from any authentic self. Furthermore, he is more rational than the violent Amphitryon, and so can find himself addressing the question of who he is in a logical, inquiring, and even philosophical way. Despite Sosia's cowardice, his double Mercury cannot quite manage to expropriate his name, and his role as "Amphitryon's man," by brute force alone. In the latter part of Act I, Scene 2, however, the god demonstrates a total knowledge of Sosia's present mission and message, his family history, his unhappy marriage, and his record of petty crimes, leading the surprised Sosia to mutter, "Except by *being* Sosia, how/Could he know so much?" Sosia then studies Mercury's person closely, finding it quite like his own, and discovers by interrogation that Mercury can remember, and claims to have done, a deed that Sosia did "when no one was around." It now seems to Sosia that he has no rational, evidential ground for denying Mercury's claim to his identity. Having made that concession, yet bothered still by the feeling that he "must be someone," Sosia struggles thereafter to maintain that there can be two Sosias in the world. Mercury, meanwhile, treats him as a nonperson who is "on standby," as we say, for an identity which he may have when Mercury is through with it.

One might gather, from what the characters are and say, that in the world of this play, old patterns of being are not viable; that identities are problematical; that the strong are cavalier and unprincipled and their inferiors debased into pawns. In any age, comedy could convert such glum premises into laughter, but they had a special pertinence and bite in Molière's day—a time, in France, of crumbling tradition and of forcefully imposed new order. Nigel Dennis' hilarious novel *Cards of Identity* had a similar pertinence to the painfully transitional state of English society after World War II.

A final concern of *Amphitryon*, and its central one, is love and marriage. Sosia has not the emotional resources for married love, while Cleanthis is starved for tenderness and soured by the want of it; the quarrelsome scenes between this couple (including the one in which Mercury plays Sosia's part) continually counterpoint the amorous dealings of their betters. Of these betters, the most complex is Jupiter. Though Mercury says that in his descents to earth, Jupiter "lays his selfhood by" (*sort tout à fait de lui-même,*) the person we meet in Act I, Scene 3 is quite simply Jupiter in disguise, pretending to be a Theban general— as Americans abroad pretend, sometimes, to be French or Italian. What this visitor seeks is sexual delight, emotional conquest, the opportunity to playact, and the connoisseur's or tourist's pleasure of sampling human feelings. This last is a chief objective when he comes onstage in Act II, Scene 4, uttering the following aside:

> I'll take this opportunity to appease
> Alcmena, and to banish her vexation,
> And in so doing taste the ecstasies
>   Of happy reconciliation.

Because Jupiter, in posing as a mortal, has taken on no human limitations, those lines are not an expression of hopeful intent but a divine fiat; the words of Jove, as he will later say, "are the decrees of Fate," and in this speech he has ordained what shall happen in the ensuing scene. Thus, there is no sincerity or suspense in his suicide threats—how could there be?—but a great deal of manipulative cruelty, since Alcmena believes him to be her husband. The purpose of his wholly theatrical behavior is to enjoy the playing of a scene, and to savor both "her young tears" and his own mastery.

The one thing in *Amphitryon* that requires a bit of historical explanation is Jupiter's insistent rigmarole about "the husband" and "the lover." Many of the *précieuses*, or bluestockings, of Molière's day had a proto-feminist disdain for the slavery of marriage, and for its sensual aspect, and cultivated (instead of marriage, or in addition to it) Platonic love-relationships of the highest spirituality and refinement. Molière's *The Learned Ladies* (1672) was to mock this separation of marriage and love, husband and lover, in its portrayal of Armande. Meanwhile, the first audience of *Amphitryon* would have been amused to hear a high-minded *précieux* distinction from one who had just accomplished a sly physical conquest. Does Jupiter suppose that his fancy talk of "husband" and "lover" will appeal to Alcmena? If so, he is, despite his omniscience, very imperceptive as to her character. What such talk clearly does reflect is Jupiter's comically balked desire to appropriate all of Alcmena's love for himself, a thing he can scarcely expect to do while disguised as Amphitryon.

We might almost think, when we first see Amphitryon with Alcmena in Act II, Scene 2, that Jupiter has preempted his "lover" side and left him nothing but "husband" qualities. He is strangely ready, from the beginning, to encounter some marital dissonance; and, hastening to mistrust his wife's fidelity, he soon arrives at the state of rage (near-tragic in its tone) that he will maintain for the rest of the play. It is a brutal rage based in part on jealousy, and to a greater extent on the loss of his honor. Since the play's action, in which he is a victim throughout, does not show us Amphitryon's more attractive aspects, we must try to remember that he is a handsome young hero, that Alcmena loves him deeply, that he must possess the charm and passion that Jove has imitated in order to deceive her, and that we, in his predicament, might do no better than he. Jules Vuillemin observes that Amphitryon's stature, far nobler than that of the usual figure of comedy, causes his absurd fate to reflect satirically on the general human condition, and on us who witness it. We glimpse in him, perhaps, our derisory relationship to forces greater than ourselves.

Amphitryon's love is possessive, in the sense that Alcmena is essential to his picture of himself. Cleanthis' needy love is also possessive in its hopeless, badgering demand that Sosia do his marital "duty." Jupiter's love—if the word applies to Jupiter at all—is ruthless, exploitative, and (strangely, since he is king of everything) self-aggrandizing. It is Alcmena who, though present in three scenes only and absent from the whole third act, is the standard whereby the play's other lovers are to be measured. She is, quite simply, a perfect wife: beautiful, modest, warm, spirited, sensible, witty, and honest; she conceives of married love as a happy mutual state in which both body and soul are given their due. She says, as Irving Singer puts it, "that she cannot and will not distinguish between lover and husband: her husband is her proper lover, and her lover must provide not only the pleasures of their mutual passion but also the goods of a married life in common." In a play full of users and used, and of manipulative lovers, Alcmena stands for the fact (as Cordelia does in *Lear*) that true and unselfish love can be.

It may seem a gross imbalance of structure that in the play's final scene Alcmena is absent and Amphitryon mute. Yet Alcmena's eloquent absence may serve to underline how little

Jupiter's "clearing of her name" could appease her horror at his cold, shallow deception. Amphitryon is speechless because, for all Jove's "sugarcoating" and grand promises, and for all his own concern with prestige and appearances, his chief reaction is that of a violent man who has been stunned by greater power. We may also read into Amphitryon's silence his response, in Act III, Scene 7, to Posicles' suggestion that Alcmena may have been quite blamelessly deceived:

> Such errors, in whatever light one views them,
>   Are bound to touch us where we live,
> And though our reason often may excuse them,
>   Our honor and our love will not forgive.

That note of inflexible resentment does not promise a quick and easy mending of Amphitryon's damaged marriage. Nor is the final scene a wholly pleasant one for Jupiter, because his jealousy of Amphitryon is real: he cannot be satisfied with his conquest of Alcmena, since the "tender love" she gave him was given, so she thought, to her husband. There are a number of closing scenes in Molière—those of *Tartuffe* and of *The School for Wives*, for instance—in which the conventional happy ending is both achieved and gently mocked; but the denouement of *Amphitryon*, repeatedly deflated by Sosia, is almost pure mockery.

The reader may wish to pursue the lover/husband notion in René Bray's *La Préciosité et les précieux*, or the dramatic history of the Amphitryon legend in Passage and Mantinband's *Amphitryon*, or other matters in the fine criticism of Lionel Gossman or J. D. Hubert. But the time has come to remember that this play made Voltaire fall over backward. The themes and behaviors I have been discussing, often in sternly judgmental words such as "amorality" and "spineless," are really there, and yet one could not possibly exaggerate the remoteness of *Amphitryon* from any spirit of preaching or censure. Whatever happens in the piece is framed in a fantasy concerning the incredible intrusions of some gods in whom we

144

do not believe, and who, as the prologue tells, are mere figments of poetic imagination. All of that distances the story from reality, gives it a fairy-tale atmosphere, and ensures that whatever dark things are said or shown will be registered, yet at the same time taken lightly. Beginning with the prologue's midair colloquy, Molière employs all means to envelop the proceedings in lightness and charm, and to that end nothing is more successful than his use of a sparkling and lyrical verse technique.

Vers libre in the French seventeenth century meant a form of poetry in which there was no prescribed rhyme scheme, and the poet could shift at will from one line length to another. This was the form employed by Molière's friend La Fontaine in his *Fables*, and, as Voltaire said, it is not as easy as it sounds. Why? Because it does not work unless there is good expressive reason for each change in line length, and unless the rhyme patterns— like the stanzas of more regular forms—embody the stages of thought. Molière's vers libre in *Amphitryon* is excellent, representing his poetry at its best and most lyric, and the reader will note the numerous ways in which this versatile form enforces one or another tone or comic effect. In many of the speeches of Jupiter and Alcmena, the baroque opulence of the rhyme combines with an artful redundancy of statement to give an impression of inexhaustible eloquence and gallantry. (The same speeches, in their leisured enlargement of a mood or idea, make one think of arias, though in 1668 the creation of French opera by Lully and Charpentier was still a few years in the future.) When virtuoso rhyme occurs in the speeches of Sosia, it has a different effect, and becomes the music of quick-witted talk or patter.

There are a variety of line lengths in Molière's text, but verses of twelve or eight syllables are the most common by far; I have tried faithfully to parallel his metrical movement in English measures. In all but one or two lines, I have been able to preserve his rhyme patterns exactly. The intended rhythms of my English lines will best be heard if the reader or actor will honor my occasional stress marks and will treat *Sosia*, *diamond*, and *hellebore* as three-syllable words.

I am indebted to J. D. McClatchy for his suggested textual changes, several of which have been gratefully made. I must also thank, in addition to my wife, William Jay Smith, Sonja Haussmann Smith, and James Merrill for counsel and/or encouragement. Finally, I am obliged to Irving Singer, who kept after me until I undertook this translation.

Richard Wilbur
Cummington, Massachusetts
June 1994